IMAGES OF IRELAND

BALLINASLOE
FROM GARBALLY PARK TO THE FAIRGREEN

IMAGES OF IRELAND

BALLINASLOE
FROM GARBALLY PARK TO THE FAIRGREEN

DECLAN KELLY

First published 2007
Reprinted 2018

The History Press Ireland
50 City Quay
Dublin 2
Ireland

www.thehistorypress.ie

© Declan Kelly, 2007

The right of Declan Kelly to be identified as the Author
of this work has been asserted in accordance with the
Copyrights, Designs and Patents Act 1988.

All rights reserved. No part of this book may be reprinted
or reproduced or utilised in any form or by any electronic,
mechanical or other means, now known or hereafter invented,
including photocopying and recording, or in any information
storage or retrieval system, without the permission in writing
from the Publishers.

British Library Cataloguing in Publication Data.
A catalogue record for this book is available from the British Library.

ISBN 978 1 84588 585 4

Typesetting and origination by The History Press
Printed by TJ International Ltd

Contents

	Author's Preface	7
one	St Grellan – Ballinasloe's First Citizen Including a Brief History of the Church	9
two	The Clancartys	23
three	Folklore, Forgotten Places and People	63

Author's Preface

As a young boy, long before the onslaught of the iPod and the Playstation, I regularly set aside one day of the week for what I innocently called 'exploring'. I was possibly a little more organised back then than I am now, and I recall making a list of all the strange and wonderful places I planned to visit. And visit them I did. At ten years of age I climbed old and dangerous stairways with a cavalier sense of disregard for personal safety. I ran like a ferret through now closed-up tunnels, my sense of awe propelling me around each new corner. Questions such as 'Who built these mysterious places?' and 'What were they like?' intrigued me, and in my mind's eye I tried to imagine them as real, flesh-and-blood people with all their joys and worries. It filled an innocent mind with wonder back then and it still does today. It was the age of Reagan and Thatcher, the Rubik's cube and Pope John Paul II, who was then at his zenith. Even the yo-yo and the hula hoop enjoyed a brief revival. Mobile phones, if they existed at all, were almost the size of cavity blocks and computers were like small Portakabins. 'Ecstasy' was sitting out on a fine sunny day and 'speed' was someone going too fast on a bicycle down Brackernagh. The 'Celtic Tiger' sounded like a sports fan with a bad hangover and the building boom was confined to modest bathroom extensions. Home furnishings were of a much simpler style then. A boiled egg and a good repast of beans for supper usually negated the need for jacuzzi baths. It seemed like an uncomplicated time but that was only from my young and innocent perspective. In reality, unemployment ran at an all-time high and parents seemed to be rearing their children for emigration. The Cold War cast a gloomy pall over the world and the Iron Curtain was tightly drawn.

We view life and its vagaries in different stages and it can often take the form of a family photo album – random snaps with some important and some not-so-important inclusions. The history of a town is something like a family photo album, with some characters and faces readily identifiable, while others have been obscured by time and failing memory; important occasions have been left unrecorded while apparently meaningless ones are given prominent placing. In the narrow confines of two hundred photographs, I have tried to capture a random glance at life in the town in which I was born and reared. Most of the 'older stock' whom I knew as a child have now gone to their reward and, while I have not lived there for some years now, the news of a local death still stirs up a sense of loneliness in me, just as the news of a local triumph awakens a sense of pride. I hope that what follows will evoke good memories for both residents past and present and even for those with no ancestral link to Ballinasloe.

My gratitude to all who have permitted me to trespass on their time for interviews and photographs and I deeply regret that I could not include all the images passed on to me.

Special thanks to long-term natives, Rory Kilduff and Joe Higgins, both of whom I have known since childhood and whose company is always a pleasure and a privilege.

Loyal friends are difficult to come by and one whose company I, and many others, have sorely missed for some time now is that of Dermot Connolly. An integral part of the town's tapestry for eighty-five years, he was one of its greatest champions. In his role as local correspondent for the *Connacht Tribune*, he went out in rain and shine to cover endless football matches. On the last occasion I saw him, he was very frail and ill but I was moved to tears because he had gone to great trouble to be with me on what was a very important day for myself and my family. Dermot embodied the true spirit of Ballinasloe and his absence from the town is incalculable. Ergo, this book is dedicated to his memory.

To Dermot Connolly (1915-2001) who was my friend.

one

St Grellan – Ballinasloe's First Citizen

Including a Brief History of the Church

On an esker near the Ahascragh boundary of the parish stands the ruin of St Grellan's church in Kilclooney. While local lore favours the opinion that the building dates back to the time of the great man himself, it is, in reality, from the late fifteenth or early sixteenth century. Doubtless, however, it occupies the site of the first Christian church in the area which was most likely constructed of wood, after the ephemeral nature of all structures of its time.

The late Monsignor Timothy Joyce recalled in his later years that an archaeologist (or, to be more precise, an Assyriologist) visited the ruins in the 1890s and claimed to have deciphered hieroglyphics on a stone. It was unlikely that this man was a 'spoofer', since he had written the article on Assyrian archaeology in the *Encyclopaedia Brittanica* of the time. Alongside Fr Joyce, he dug in the doorway and, comparing the depth of the floor surface to the surface level of that time, estimated the building to be about three thousand years old. He further concluded that it pre-dated the time of St Grellan and may once have been a pagan building. Current archaeological knowledge proves this cannot be so, though one may speculate that Grellan, perhaps, chose to found his church on an already-established site of pagan worship. This scholarly gentleman probably also overlooked the fact that continuous burials would have led to an accumulation of earth in the graveyard which would have raised the ground much faster.

Kilclooney church is beautifully simplistic. The windows follow no specific type of design and, while the door is pointed in accordance with Gothic architecture, there are no other traces of this style to be found in the building.

It is recorded in *The Life of St Grellan* that his birth was preceded by a violent thunderstorm and that he acted as an intermediary between the Firbolgs and the hosts of Máine who had come from the modern Clogher in Tyrone to demand that tribute and territory be paid to them. Cian of the Firbolgs assembled his hosts to the number of three thousand and set out to meet the invaders who were encamped in Druim Clasagh between Lough Ree and the River Suck – probably the modern Drum – in a plain known as Tír Máine.

It was shown to St Grellan that the race of Colla Da Chrioch were in peril, and the saint came speedily to protect them. He repressed both parties, checked their animosity and ratified a peace between them, ordering that three times nine of their nobility should be given into the hands of the Firbolgs as a pledge to observe this peace. Amlaigh, the son of Máine, was thus delivered into the hands of the Firbolg lawgiver, whose wife fell in love with him. The lawgiver was filled with jealousy and hatred and induced Cian, the Firbolg chief, to murder all the hostages. To complete the perfidious proceeding, Cian invited the Colla Da Chrioch chiefs to a feast. His real intention was to ambush them while they were en route and kill every last one of them. The Colla Da Chrioch, who were encamped at a place called Seisidh Beag, had to cross the Fohenagh bog to get to the feast. It was in this bog that Cian and his men were stationed. The vigilant St Grellan, however, spotted the ambuscade from the doorway of his church in Kilclooney and, divining foul play in the offing, raised his hands to heaven and beseeched the Lord to intercept this calamity. Immediately, the bog opened and, in a retribution of biblical proportions, the entire ambuscade were swallowed whole, leaving no survivors to tell the tale. Afterwards this place received the name the Plain of Sorrow. Furthermore, a local legend held that the seven churches were to be built by the well under the shadow of the present ruin, but the monks were interrupted in their work by a woman who came to the well.

St Grellan's Well was once a site of devotion and stations were performed there regularly. Each pilgrim always left something after them at the well as a gift or token. A 'pattern' was held at the well every 17 September but local clergy forbade the practice after abuses crept in and this date became the occasion of excessive drinking and carousing. A pattern hasn't been held there since sometime in the late 1870s.

The 'Bachall Griollain'

Of the saint's wooden staff or crozier we know very little outside of that it was handed down from John O'Donovan, the nineteenth-century scholar. A treasured relic of the Hymany people, it was handed down from one hereditary custodian to the next and was kept in a crozier shrine of bronze. Believed locally to have been possessed of divine powers, it was often used in the swearing of oaths. However, it was lost in the 1830s when, according to local lore, a Mrs Rogers threw it in a river following a disagreement with the Parish Priest of Ahascragh.

'The Teampoilín'

On the eastern end of the old Grand Canal, about one mile from Ballinasloe, stands the ruins of an old church known as 'the Teampoilín' or 'little temple'. An old wooden roadway, or *togher*, once connected this church to the Abbey of Clontuskert and facilitated the canons regular of St Augustine in the holding of divine services at this spot. The walls of huge stones comprising the remains of the church are held together by 'ox-blood' mortar and are built on a plinth of massive stones. Gothic in style, it dates from the early thirteenth century, making it the earliest extant church or building in Ballinasloe. In less enlightened times it was used as a burial place for unbaptised babies.

Creagh

The proper designation of the parish is 'Kilclooney and Creagh', though it is sometimes erroneously called 'the parish of Ballinasloe'. The present town is relatively modern in comparison to the old parishes. Kilclooney and Creagh were united at an uncertain date in the early eighteenth century due to the shortage of clergy and financial support created by penal enactments. Very little information exists about the parish of Creagh. It is bounded on the west by the River Suck and covers an area of about fifteen square miles. As recently as the 1930s it was sparsely populated but, at that time, the many ruined farmhouses that peppered the area bore sad testimony to the ravages of famine and landlordism. In recent years, Creagh has undergone something of a rebirth and is again a densely populated part of the town. The parish joins Taughmaconnell on the north-eastern extremity and Moore on the southern and eastern side.

Moore

The parish of Moore, in the archdiocese of Tuam, protrudes geographically into the parish of Ballinasloe. It is an 'island' parish, with a portion of Creagh also completely enclosed by it. This unusual portion starts at the top of Kilbegley Hill and advances towards the River Suck in a narrowing strip. The locals believe that Moore remains attached to Tuam because a former abbot of Clonmacnoise, who was once 'parochus' or Parish Priest of this territory, became Bishop of Tuam. He retained his parochial territory with its right of way to the Shannon. As a result of some compromise, he permitted the alienation of the island portion now belonging to Creagh, while he retained his right to the richer lands lying around the ancient church of St Begley.

There is, however, no documentary evidence to support this story. Local lore has it that the first church in Creagh was built by St Patrick, who, having crossed the Shannon, laid a foundation somewhere in this area. Most likely it was built by 'disciples of his disciples', as it were, given the huge number of 'St Patrick's Wells' dotted around the whole of Ireland.

In the area of the town cemetery stand the ruins of three churches. Overlooking the road at what for many years has been called 'Staunton's Corner' is the ruin of an early eighteenth-century church used for Protestant worship before the building of St John's church. It does, however, stand on the site of the old parish church of Creagh.

The second ruin is of a small 'mass cabin' or 'mass chapel', dating from penal days. The late Very Revd Dr Kevin Egan dated this tiny structure to c. 1702 and it served the parish until a more adequate building was erected in 1824. This newer building, now mostly levelled, was initiated by Archdeacon Laurence Dillon, who, towards the end of his life, began his most ambitious project – the building of St Michael's church. Old photographs reveal the 1824 church to be a somewhat crude structure, predominantly Gothic with its roof supported by stone columns of rubble masonry, plastered and painted. These columns supported arches on which a main beam of masonry was sprung to support the roof. Within the church lie the remains of the Venerable Archdeacon Dillon and also those of Dr Thomas Costello, Bishop of the diocese of Clonfert from 1787 to 1831. This church was unique in that, up until the early 1940s, it contained the only extant example of a penal altar, bearing the inscription:

> Pray for M. Anthony and Mrs Catherine Brabazon who caused this Altar to be erected April the 2nd 1756.

Sadly, this unique object of veneration has vanished, undoubtedly vandalised for its stone slabs, sometime in the early 1960s. Nor indeed does the story end there, for a mere twenty years earlier, the wall slabs marking the graves of Bishop Costello, Archdeacon Laurence Dillon and his nephew, Fr Gerard Dillon, were stolen in a similar fashion.

St Michael's

The former parish church which replaced the foundation of Kilclooney stood within the site of the present St Michael's in the Market Square. The Venerable Archdeacon Dillon began to make preparations for the building of the church in 1847. Tradition has it that he applied to the 3rd Earl of Clancarty for a site and the Earl referred him to his agent, Admiral Trench. The latter refused his request, whereupon (lore has it) he began to lose his sight. When the Earl heard of the refusal and its consequences, he sent for Fr Dillon and offered him a site anywhere he wished to build. Fr Dillon selected the present site and had it granted to him on the condition that the frontage was not to extend beyond a certain point. Hence, the local belief that Clancarty would grant only the bed of a river as a site for St Michael's church.

Yet another tradition holds that Clancarty stood at the top of the Square and fired a stone, decreeing that wheresoever it landed, Dillon could have his church. Given that the Earl was, by the 1840s, at the zenith of his family's powers and that a church already stood on the banks of the River Suck, we can discount this tradition as merely apocraphyl. In any event, for the stone to have landed at the present site, the Earl would have needed a stronger arm than that of an Olympian.

St Michael's stands on the eastern bank of the River Suck and was built by designs belonging to McCarthy, which were then revised by the celebrated Augustus Welby Pugin. The style is decorated Gothic. The aisles are separated from the nave (the central part of the church) by stone pillars, from which spring out stone arches. The design of the apse window reputedly mirrors the design of that in the Franciscan priory at Kilconnell. The altar is the work of Albert Power of Dublin who was very friendly with Fr James Madden, Adm., (1920-1928).

The church was consecrated in 1858 by Dr John Derry, Bishop of Clonfert, who had grown up on Dunlo Street where his father, Michael, ran a pub and grocery. The parish registers date from 1820.

Older Schools in Ballinasloe

Even as far back as 1931, no resident of Kilclooney could recall there being a hedge school in the area, surmising that perhaps it came too close to the Clancarty home. In 1931, however, an older resident of Kilclooney, who attended the Protestant school in Brackernagh, recounted an interesting story. He claimed there was no religious instruction whatsoever during the day, but that last thing in the afternoon the master would give the pupils a few verses to learn from the Bible.

This same resident also narrated an incident about the efforts of Fr Patrick Costello, Adm., to get the Catholic children of the town to go to their own schools. The Revd John Cottonwalker was the local Church of Ireland minister and did not see eye to eye, as it were, with Fr Costello. On one occasion, Fr Costello went to the Brackernagh school and ordered all the Catholic children to leave. They promptly obeyed, but before Fr Costello could leave the grounds of the school, the Revd Mr Cottonwalker appeared before him. After an exchange of 'compliments', Cottonwalker challenged Costello to a debate on sacred scripture.

By now, word had spread of the verbal battle royal taking place in the grounds of the school and it appears that all the workers in the Brackernagh quarries – stone-cutters, dressers and breakers – came down en masse, carrying their implements to defend Fr Costello if the need arose. Fr Costello bade them return to their work and told Cottonwalker he would be 'fixed up' before the week was out. The same elderly resident of Kilclooney claimed that, on that very day week, he himself attended Cottonwalker's funeral and walked with it 'to a grave on Kilclooney Hill'. Legends abound about Fr Costello and, even as late as the 1950s, when Dr Egan was writing his book on Ballinasloe, elderly residents still had vivid recollections of him.

On another occasion, he is reputed to have been walking down a street in the town when he passed Cottonwalker travelling in the opposite direction. The latter stuck out his tongue at him whereupon Fr Costello put a 'curse' on him and Cottonwalker could not pull his tongue back in for the rest of his days.

Yet another tale relates how Fr Costello was summoned by the Dowager Clancarty who complained that the convent bell disturbed her sleep. Fr Costello pretended to take her grievance into consideration and promised to have it remedied the following morning. When morning came, the Dowager was stone deaf!

As apocryphal as all these stories are, it cannot be denied that Costello was a strong personality in Ballinasloe. He was responsible for the building of the spire of St Michael's and later, when he went to Woodford, he actively helped in constructing the village's roads that ran into the mountains. He died in 1901 and is buried in St Brendan's church, Looscaun.

There was a hedgeschool in Coilean or Castlepark at which a Gately was the master. There was, also in the '30s, a cave on Coilean Hill said to have been put there by the Norsemen. It was more likely a souterrain.

Mass Rocks

There were two known mass rocks in Ballinasloe: one in the field bordering the road on the left as one turns down to Newtown school, the other in Killahornia wood. Of the latter, it was held that in this wood an old man, who was a spy, had put out his hands as a signal to his covert employees and was stuck to a tree by the Lord. This incident is mentioned in connection with the O'Shaughnessy family of Birchgrove House who allegedly converted to Catholicism following the miracle.

Attyrory

A Miss Kelly ran a Bible school in Attyrory back in the 1860s and McDonald, a former sometimes under-secretary for Ireland, was born in Attyrory House. In Woodmount, a Matty Killian had another Bible school.

Castlepark

A Lady Muldoon lived in a castle in this village and it is said that the ghosts of yeomen are sometimes seen sowing crops in the castle field. A legend about a crock of gold being buried under the site of the castle was prevalent until the 1930s.

Right: An impression of the head of the hallowed St Grellan, in Finnure cemetery chapel, Mullagh (near Loughrea). 'Grellan' is still a common Christian name in parts of County Roscommon. *(Photo courtesy of Fr Declan Kelly, private collection)*

Below middle: 'The Teampoilín', Poolboy. *(Photo courtesy of Clonfert Diocesan Archive)*

Below: 1702 Mass Chapel, Creagh cemetery; the first recorded Parish Priest of 'Kilclooney and Creagh', Fr Thomas Kenny, is interred here. He died in 1792. From the twelfth to the sixteenth century the spiritual needs of the people of the parish were tended to by the canons regular of St Augustine. *(Photo courtesy of Clonfert Diocesan Archive)*

The Brabazon Altar in the 1824 Creagh church. It originally stood in the nearby Mass Chapel of 1702, and was added to at later dates. The inscription reads:

IMI
Pray for Mr Anthony and Mrs Catherine Brabazon
who caused this altar to be erected April the 2nd 1756.

Made of local limestone, it had a white appearance due to having been painted. It was removed by 'persons unknown' in the 1960s. *(Photo courtesy of Clonfert Diocesan Archive)*

Above left: Ornate head, detail from Kilclooney church. *(Photo courtesy of Fr Declan Kelly, private collection)*

Above right: C. 1960, St Michael's church with the imposing spire built by Fr Costello, Adm. *(Photo courtesy of Clonfert Diocesan Archive)*

The pre-conciliar interior of St Michael's church. The pulpit was dismantled in the late 1960s and remoulded into a baptismal font. The inscription on it dedicates it to Fr Patrick Costello, Adm., of the parish (1882-1889). Costello, who came from Leitrim parish, was an austere but extremely energetic man and completed the building of the church spire in 1887. The high altar was designed and executed by Albert Power. Using Connemara marble, it incorporates the image of the dead Christ. An accidental fire in 2001 closed the church for a year and a half, but it reopened in December 2002. St Michael's also contains two windows by Harry Clarke, depicting St Patrick and St Rose of Lima. *(Photo courtesy of Clonfert Diocesan Archive)*

This fine building is St John's church which serves the Church of Ireland. Overlooking the Fair Green, it is built on the hill of Knockadoon, which, from its appearance, gives the impression of a motte and bailey. St John's was built in 1843. *(Photo courtesy of Theo Hanley)*

Above: View of St Michael's Square, or the Market Place, from the late nineteenth century. *(Photo courtesy of Clonfert Diocesan Archive)*

Left: Dr John Derry (1811-1870) who became Bishop of Clonfert in 1847. He was reared on Dunlo Street in a small grocery, owned by his father Michael, opposite where St Michael's Presbytery stands today. He spent a short time as Junior Dean in Maynooth seminary, returning to become Parish Priest of Ballymacward. The building of St Michael's Church, Ballinasloe, was begun by Archdeacon Dillon in Dr Derry's time and it was he who invited Cardinal Wiseman to the town for the solemn consecration on 25 August 1858. Derry's relations with the Clancarty family were strained, to put it mildly, having clashed with them over the question of religion being taught in schools on their estates. Although he was brought up in Ballinasloe, Dr Derry was born in the hermitage parish of Moore. A brother, William, became Parish Priest of Eyrecourt. *(Photo courtesy of Fr Declan Kelly, private collection)*

Nicholas Cardinal Wiseman (1802-1865). He arrived in Ballinasloe for the solemn consecration of St Michael's church on 24 August 1858 and received a tumultuous welcome. Halfway into the town, the horses were unbridled from his coach and it was drawn triumphantly through the streets by notables of the town. The following day he preached at 11 a.m. Mass following the consecration. It is estimated that 20,000 to 25,000 people flocked to the town for an occasion that was unparalleled in history. Wiseman, who was of Irish parentage himself, was the first head of the newly restored English hierarchy in 1850. During his brief visit to the town, he was a guest of Gill's Hotel. Also attending the event was one of Emperor Napoleon III's chaplains, the Abbé Cruise of Paris. *(Photo courtesy of Clonfert Diocesan Archive)*

The cenotaph on Dunlo Hill – erected in memory of Archdeacon Charles Le Poer Trench who died in 1839. *(Photo courtesy of Theo Hanley)*

Left: Monsignor Timothy Joyce (1868-1947) in typically regal pose. A native of Portumna, he brought about many improvements in Ballinasloe while acting as parish administrator, beautifying the Market Square and purchasing the old agricultural hall for the parish, which had been built in 1846 by the 3rd Earl of Clancarty. He had been the favourite of the clergy to succeed Dr O'Doherty as Bishop of Clonfert in 1923, but O'Doherty favoured Dignan, who cycled from Killimor to the Bishop's house in Loughrea to be informed of Rome's decision. 'What should I do?' asked Fr Dignan. 'Accept it, of course', came the reply. Joyce served as Vicar-General of the diocese of Clonfert from 1919. His remains were recently exhumed and re-interred in the grounds of the newer church of St Brigid in Portumna. In 1904 and 1905 he absented himself from the town to raise funds for the building of a cathedral in Loughrea. *(Photo courtesy of Fr Declan Kelly, private collection)*

Below: The funeral of Monsignor Joyce in Portumna, February 1947. *(Photo courtesy of Fr Brendan Lawless)*

Above: The funeral of Monsignor Joyce in Portumna, February 1947. *(Photo courtesy of Fr Brendan Lawless)*

Below: St Gabriel's Convent, c.1960. *(Photo courtesy of Clonfert Diocesan Archive)*

Left: Fr John Bowes (1866-1937) who was Adm. in Ballinasloe from 1893 to 1901. He built St Michael's Presbytery in 1894, the priests of the town having to take lodgings prior to that. The presbytery is located on the old site of Brutin's Yard on Dunlo Street. A native of Caheronaun, Loughrea, his first cousins, Fr Thomas and Fr Bernard Bowes, were also priests of Clonfert diocese. Fr John Fahy (1893-1969), his nephew, became a noted Republican sympathiser and founded Lia Fáil. Fr John Bowes went to Woodford as Parish Priest in 1901, and spent his final years there invalided. *(Photo courtesy of Fr Declan Kelly, private collection)*

Below: Our Lady of Lourdes church, Creagh, c.1960. *(Photo courtesy of Clonfert Diocesan Archive)*

two

The Clancartys

Without any doubt, the most important family name in the history of the town of Ballinasloe is that of 'Clancarty'. In the eighteenth and nineteenth centuries, the Clancartys exerted enormous influence on religious matters, the development of the town and the Great Fair, the improvement of local agriculture and the material prosperity of their tenantry.

The Trenches were a French Huguenot family who had settled in England. They first appeared in Ireland in 1605 in the person of James Trench, a Protestant minister. James married Margaret, the daughter of Lord Viscount Montgomery of Aides, and was presented with the rectory of Clongell in Co. Meath. The first member of the family to settle in Garbally is said to have been Frederick Trench, who married his first cousin, Anne (daughter of James) in 1632.

James had purchased much land in Cavan and further purchases were made there by Frederick. His interest in Garbally castle and lands is also said to have arisen by purchase, but was confirmed by patent from Charles II. Frederick died in 1669. His son, who was also called Frederick, was born in 1633, succeeded his father at Garbally and added to the estate by purchase in 1678. The land thus acquired comprised the whole parish of Kilclooney, including the present town of Ballinasloe and a large area in the parish of Clontuskert.

How these lands became available to the Trenches has never been fully explained, but some understanding of the situation can be gathered. At the Composition of Connaught in 1585, an area on either side of the River Suck, comprising roughly the parishes of Kilclooney and Creagh and perhaps of Clontuskert and Ahascragh, was described as 'Clonmacnowen'.

In 1583, the Earl of Clanricard owned the castle of Ballinasloe and a quarter of the lands there. Sir Anthony Brabazon, Governor of Connaught in the late sixteenth century, lived at Ballinasloe and doubtless held some land in the vicinity. His grandson, Anthony, converted to Catholicism, joined in the rebellion of 1641 and was excluded from pardon by the Cromwellians. Doubtless both they and the O'Kellys were deprived of land at that period. By the Cromwellian Settlement, the barony of Moycarn (including the parish of Creagh) was in theory set aside for Cork and Wexford inhabitants and that of Clonmacnowen for Carlow, Waterford and Limerick. But if any of the transplanted came, they have left no trace. We can only conclude that some of the O'Kelly, Brabazon or Clanricard lands were confiscated and assigned to persons removed to Connaught and that these persons (unwilling or unable to claim their lands) sold them to Frederick Trench as did the Esmondes and the Eyres of nearby Eyrecourt. These lands were doubtless bought for a song. Two and six or five shillings an acre was the common asking price.

Thus, Frederick Trench found himself a substantial landowner but lacking in any political importance. His brother, John, was a minister. Their great opportunity came during the Williamite War. John had been the source of much useful information – even crossing to England in May 1690 with others, in an open boat, to give full particulars of conditions in Ireland to King William. Fate willed it that the line of retreat from Athlone passed through Ballinasloe, and the Battle of Aughrim was fought in sight of the hills of Garbally. Frederick Trench, according to his own family tradition, turned his house into a hospital and opened the doors to the Williamites. He and John gave active assistance on the day of the battle, pointing out the pass where the Williamites were enabled to attack the left flank of the Irish Army. For his services, John was made Dean of Raphoe and was the ancestor of the Barons Ashtown. Frederick Trench's son, Frederick, who succeeded to Garbally on his father's death in 1704, became, politically, one of the strongest men in County Galway. In 1703, he was high sheriff of the county and by 1715 he was colonial commandant of one of the regiments of the military dragoons there; in that same year he became one of the knights of the shire for County Galway, and he held this post until his death in 1752. His son, Richard, who had already succeeded in 1734, sat in parliament for the borough of Banagher, and, from 1761 to 1768, was a knight of the shire of County Galway. In 1732, he married Frances, the only daughter of David Power of Coorheen, and through her the Trench family acquired all the Power estates in the baronies of Leitrim, Dunkellin and Loughrea, as well as the Keating estates in Kilkenny, Carlow and Dublin, which Frances had inherited from her mother.

The Power alliance was one of great consequence for the Trench family, for in addition to the vast increase in wealth, it gave them connections to ancient Norman and Irish nobility. Her father, David Power of Coorheen, was a descendant of the Norman, Sir Geoffrey Le Poer of Dunisle in County Cork, and their Cromwellian grant in County Galway may have been a revival of the original grant of Klamoy in the barony of Leitrim to Eustace Le Poer, the Munster Baron in 1301. The great-great-grandmother of Frances was the daughter of Cormac MacCarthy, Viscount Muskerry, a descendant of Dermot MacCarthy Mór, King of Munster and a sister of Donough, the 2nd Earl of Clancartie [sic], who was outlawed at the time of Charles II. On the basis of that connection, the earldom of Clancarty was regranted to the Trench family after the Union. Richard Trench died in 1768 and was succeeded by his son William, who, in the same year, had been elected knight of the shire for County Galway and was also appointed one of the governors of the county. He served in parliament until 1797, voting at first with the Whigs but switching over to Pitt in about 1791. In 1797, he was made Baron Kilconnell of Garbally.

His son, Richard, was born in 1767, educated at Cambridge and called to the Bar in 1793, becoming an MP for County Galway in 1797. In 1796, he married Harriette Staples, daughter of John Staples of Lissane in County Tyrone and a relation of the Earl of Castlereagh. In 1799, he voted against the Union but, in 1800, he voted for it, influenced, it was said, by Castlereagh and the promise of an earldom. As has previously been mentioned, his father had already been made a Baron and now, in return for Frederick's vote, he was rapidly promoted to Viscount Dunlo (1801) and Earl of

Clancarty (1803). He died in 1805. It was not, however, until 1823, that Frederick, 2nd Earl of Clancarty, was made a peer of the United Kingdom.

Thus, within two hundred years, the family who had set out with the humble parson of Clongell, succeeded in reaching the highest ranks of the peerage. They achieved this through acquisition of confiscated lands, judicious marriage alliances and, indeed, to some extent, good luck. The Cromwellian confiscation gave them their first opportunity. Their adherence to the Williamite cause gave them preferment. Frances Power of Coorheen brought wealth and a semblance of ancient nobility while the alliance with Castlereagh at the Union won them an earldom. But there was more to come.

The Union marked the beginning of a successful political career for Richard Trench, Viscount Dunlo and the Earl of Clancarty. He became a commissioner for the affairs of India (1807-1809) and a representative peer from 1808 until the time of his death. He also served as Master of the Mint (1812-1814) and president of the Board of Trade (1812-1818). When the Prince of Orange became King of the Netherlands, he was made ambassador to The Hague from 1813 to 1823. In 1814, he was one of England's plenipotentiaries to the Congress of Vienna. In 1818, he was appointed Marquess of Heusden in the Netherlands and received an annual pension of £2,000. Returning from the embassy of The Hague in 1823, he received a viscountcy of the UK and died in 1837.

In Richard, 2nd Earl of Clancarty, the Garbally family found their most remarkable member and reached the zenith of their power. It was Richard who built Garbally House and, in his time, the town of Ballinasloe developed and the estates thereabout benefited from great improvements. His second brother, Power Le Poer Trench, largely through his influence, became the Protestant Archbishop of Tuam. Another brother, William, became a vice admiral. His fourth brother was Charles Le Poer Trench, Archdeacon of Ardagh, whom the cenotaph on Dunlo Hill commemorates.

After his time, the earls of Clancarty created no other stirrings in the political world. They remained, for the most part of that century, gentlemen with a reputation for moderation when dealing with their dependants. In the management of their estates, they encouraged the development of agriculture, the improvement of livestock and the betterment of their tenantry. Thomas, the 3rd Earl, was born in 1803, married Sarah Juliana, daughter of the 3rd Earl of Carrick, and died in 1872. His son, Richard, was born in 1834, married Georgina, daughter of the 2nd Marquess of Bristol, and died in 1891.

At this time, the considerable wealth of the Clancartys began to disappear. By 1883, the Earl's estate amounted to 23,896 acres in County Galway and 1,614 in County Roscommon, with rental costing £12,817 a year. The 3rd Earl's will was proven at £39,739. When the 5th Earl succeeded in 1891, the net annual income from the estate was only £4,000. The land agitation and subsequent land acts added to his difficulties. He was declared bankrupt in Ireland in June 1907 and in England in August 1910. The 5th Earl's marriage was, in part, responsible for this calamity. Born in 1868, he got married in 1889 while still a minor. His wife was Isabel Bilton (Belle Bilton), an actress at the Empire Theatre and daughter of George Bilton, an assistant at Woolrich Dockyard. His father was incensed by what he considered a highly unsuitable marriage and did everything he could to have it dissolved but he failed and, in his anger, he disposed of all the family wealth that lay within his power. The marriage was a happy one but the family had been reduced to poverty. Tradition in Ballinasloe holds that, upon his return to take possession of the family seat, the 5th Earl and his bride were forced to scale the walls of Garbally Park as the gates had been locked. In 1922, the house and park were sold to the diocese of Clonfert for £6,750, and the Trench connection with Ballinasloe came to an end. The estates were taken over by the Land Commission and divided among the tenants. The 5th Earl died of influenza in 1929; his wife had died of cancer over twenty years previously. Both he and his wife, however, were remembered with great affection by the people of the town.

Loyalty and Courage

The motto of St Joseph's Diocesan College, 'Fide Et Fortitudine', was an apt choice, for the establishment's decision to move in 1923 was somewhat bold. Since the turn of the century the college had been located at an area in the townland of Creagh known as The Pines. Though a fine and imposing building housed the college there, the acquisition of the former mansion seat of the Clancartys, complete with its extensive grounds, presented far more possibilities in terms of residential facilities for boarding pupils, recreation space and, vitally, room to build class halls for future generations of students. In its new location, the first president was Fr Thomas Dempsey. A native of the parish of Kiltullagh, Dempsey was a mild-mannered, academic man and, while he provided a steady hand for the helm, Garbally College, as it would come to be known, needed a person of greater drive and vision. It was to find such traits in Fr James Cogavin.

Assuming the presidency in 1924, when Fr Dempsey joined the staff of UCG, Cogavin wasted no time in effecting the necessary changes to the aging house. It was his intention to place the establishment on a par with any of the other colleges and he succeeded in so doing. Rugby was made a priority sport (without Gaelic games being neglected), the college began to produce annual operas from the Gilbert and Sullivan canon (much in-line with the fashion of the time) and, after a few years, the college produced *Gearrbhaile*, the only all-Irish magazine from a secondary school at that time. Cogavin was fortunate in that he had the full support of all the dignitaries of the diocese. Dr John Dignan, the newly appointed Bishop of Clonfert, had been a student of the old college of Esker and had a deep and abiding interest in education and the Irish language. The Vicar General, Monsignor Timothy Joyce, was a native of the diocese and had helped lay the groundwork for the acquisition of Garbally Park. Working together, Cogavin provided the gravitas and energy, Dignan the financial and moral support and Joyce the charm. None of these men possessed a vaulting sense of ambition, all were brother priests first and foremost and were passionately loyal to the diocese of Clonfert. Prior to 1923, boarding pupils were drawn primarily from the somewhat narrow pool of the parishes of the diocese. As the college's reputation grew, they began to come from all over the country.

Cogavin threw himself into his role with gusto and ensured that only the most up-to-date lighting and heating systems were installed with proper sanitation facilities. He was not unaided by the picturesque setting of the college, surrounded as it was by wood and glade. In point of fact, it was set in 250 acres of woodland.

Hot lunches were served at 12.30 p.m. and a three-course dinner at 3.15 p.m. every day; later, when the revolving doors were installed at the front of the main house, a student was heard to bemoan that 'it'd be more in his line to spend the money on rashers!' Fr Cogavin was to remain as president until 1944, guiding the college through the lean years of the Second World War. In that same year, he became Parish Priest of Eyrecourt.

'The Opera'

One of the high points of the college year was the annual Christmas 'opera'. It was Fr Cogavin who introduced it, even going as far as to bring one Lionel Cranfield down from Dublin to take advantage of his experience working with the Rathmines and Rathgar Musical Society. Cranfield versed the students in the finer points of D'oyly Carte Opera Co. stage movement. In recent years, and more especially since the lapse of copyright on Gilbert and Sullivan works in 1961, some light-opera aficionados have ridiculed the older stage methods. But such blinkered thinking masquerading as artistic liberalism fails to grasp the basic concept, i.e. that the whole is always greater than the part. Cogavin adopted the same view where his college was concerned, and so he drafted in the services of a unique lady for musical direction, Lavinia Sheridan, L.I.S.M., more commonly known as 'Breezy'. (She had often assailed the chorister pumping the church organ bellows with cries of 'More breeze! More breeze, Sir!') She became an institution in herself in both Garbally and Ballinasloe. By the time of her death in 1972, she had outlived virtually all of her contemporaries. Breezy had spent her early career in Germany as musical instructress to the children of a German baron and had travelled the continent. She was initially dubious of the prospect of 'a bunch of kids… doing an opera?' but Cogavin was undeterred. He gathered a group of students in a room, placed a score of HMS *Pinafore* in front of one Billy Holmes, who was seated at a piano, and ordered him to play. Working next door, Miss Sheridan was horrified at the version she heard of 'Over the Bright Blue Sea'. By the end of the day, she was in charge and, on 18 May 1927, she conducted the first college opera in the town hall. In 1940, Cogavin built the College Concert Hall, which was christened with a production of *The Mikado*, a show which, happily, was Breezy's favourite.

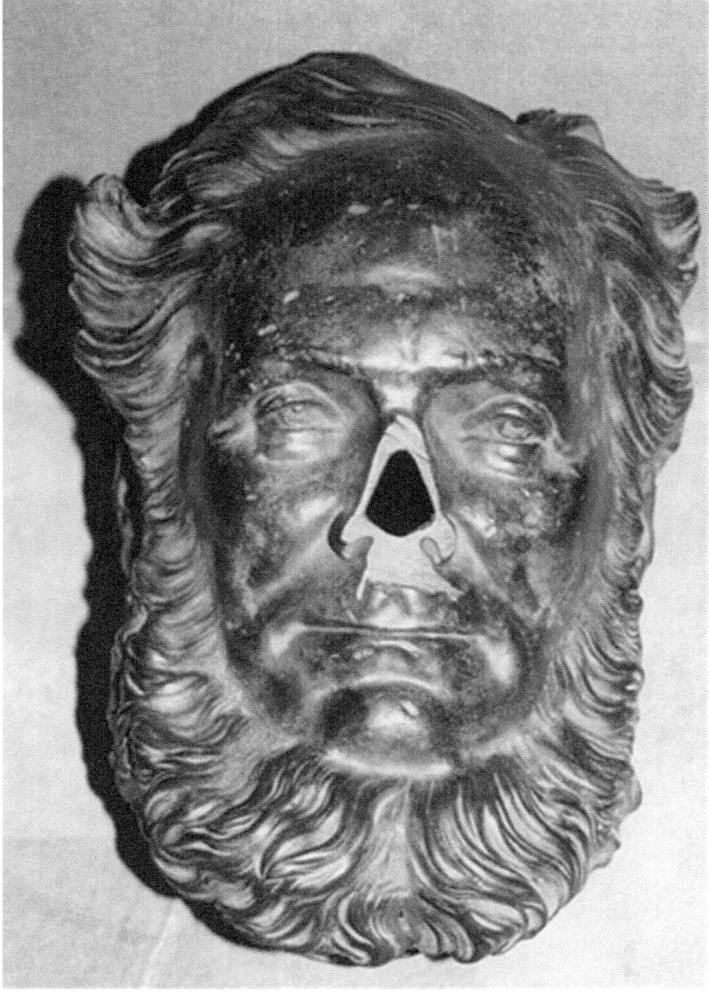

Above: The imposing Garbally House, built by the 2nd Earl of Clancarty. The road veering to the left brings one to the 'Broad Walk' and to an 'ice-house', the Victorian answer to our modern deep freeze! *(Photo courtesy of Clonfert Diocesan Archive)*

Left: 'Bring me the head of the 3rd Earl…' The last remaining portion of the statue of Thomas Le Poer Trench, 3rd Earl of Clancarty (1803-1872), which stood on Sarsfield Road. In 1921, local Republicans (believed to have been led by Jack Keogh) decapitated the statue and mutilated the nose, throwing it through the shop window of a local family. In the late 1950s, the pedestal and body portion of the statue were dismantled and taken away. The 'head of the Earl' is now in the possession of Garbally College. *(Photo courtesy of Theo Hanley)*

'The King who never came…' A room truly fit for a king and appropriately named 'The Throne Room'. It was specially designed by the 2nd Earl, complete with a throne, in the hope that George IV, King of England (1820-1830), would visit. He never did. Nonetheless, a large portrait of him adorns the dining room of Garbally House, much to the chagrin of the late Fr John Fahy, a noted patriot. The 'throne' is no longer on display. Fr Cogavin considered it unsuitable that it be kept in a Catholic college and Bishop Dignan, whose life had once been threatened by Crown forces, was in agreement. Ergo, in the mid-twenties it was removed to the backyard where students kicked it asunder in jig-time. *(Photo courtesy of Theo Hanley)*

Lady Dunlo or 'Belle Bilton': the 5th Earl's marriage to the former music-hall actress enraged his father so much that he tried to disinherit him through impoverishment. But their love won out and Belle Bilton endeared herself to the people of the town through her goodness and simplicity. It is said that she once displayed her contempt for local gentry (who privately sneered at her lowly origins) by performing a ballet for them in the dining hall, raising her bejewelled feet as high as the ornate candelabra. The 5th Earl looked on in amusement as the audience squirmed uncomfortably in their seats. Lady Dunlo died from stomach cancer while only in her late thirties but, for many years afterwards, the people of the town remembered her fondly for her many kindnesses. *(Photo courtesy of Clonfert Diocesan Archive)*

St Michael's on Market Square, taken c. 1900. Two women chatting over a fruit and vegetable stand are the sole occupants of this scene on what appears to have been a quiet day for business. Prominent in the photograph are the old market house built by the 2nd Earl of Clancarty in 1824, a monument and a weigh-bridge. In September 1918, Fr Timothy Joyce had all of these structures removed with great alacrity as they were blocking the view of his church and the entrance to the Square. The Market House held bad memories for the townspeople because in October 1826 it had been the location of a police-orchestrated physical assault on several of the town's leading Catholic gentry. *(Photo courtesy of Clonfert Diocesan Archive)*

Above left: Portrait of Monsignor James Madden (1830-1901) which hangs in Garbally House. Monsignor Madden was Vicar General of Clonfert diocese and it was through the generosity of the Madden family that a diocesan college was enabled. The family's link with the college has continued to the present day. *(Photo courtesy of Theo Hanley)*

Above right: Dr George Madden (died 1961) who was a student of the old diocesan college of Esker. *(Photo courtesy of Chrissie Robinson)*

Right: Mrs Madden, sister-in-law of Monsignor James and mother of Fr John. *(Photo courtesy of Chrissie Robinson)*

Below left: Polly (Mary Anne) Madden, Fr John's sister, who lived in London with her mother. She died unmarried in 1934. *(Photo courtesy of Chrissie Robinson)*

Below right: Fr Patrick Connolly, SSC, (1886-1945), who was instrumental in the purchase of Garbally Park as a diocesan college. A native of Ahascragh, he was ordained in 1911 for the diocese of Clonfert but later joined the fledgling Maynooth Mission to China. In some respects austere, he was a well-liked confessor to students on his visits to the college and influenced many in their decision to join the Columban Order. He had a large part to play in Fr Peter Greaney's vocation. *(Photo courtesy of Clonfert Diocesan Archive)*

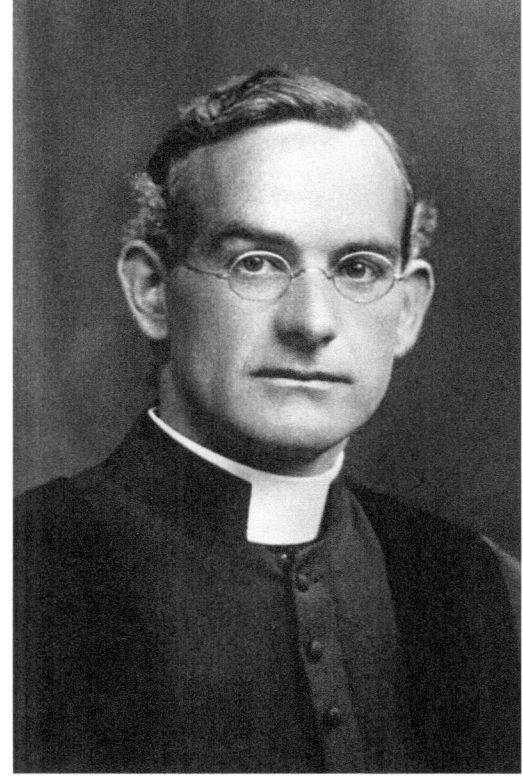

The Pines which served as the diocesan college from 1900 to 1923. Later, it belonged to St Brigid's Hospital. It is now a residential area. *(Photo courtesy of Garbally College Archives)*

Knuckling down... the old study hall in 1924. *(Photo courtesy of Garbally College Archives)*

Right: Four of the survivors of the Cartron House class of 1892 (pictured in 1942): Fr Heagney, Mr Royston, Bishop Dignan, Fr Madden. *(Photo courtesy of Garbally College Archives)*

Below: Formerly the House Stables and now class halls, the windows in these buildings were replaced in 1975. *(Photo courtesy of Garbally College Archives)*

The oratory at Garbally, taken c. 1924. This beautifully ornate, barrel-shaped room was originally the ballroom and art gallery, built c. 1855. At the uppermost level was a viewing balcony, now walled-off. *(Photo courtesy of Garbally College Archives)*

Gymnastics 1932-1933. Standing fourth from left is Reggie Bowes, a boarder from Loughrea, who died while serving with the RAF in the Second World War. Seventh and last from the left is Aidan Cusack, who became a Cistercian and president of Mount St. Joseph, Roscrea. *(Photo courtesy of Garbally College Archives)*

The names of all these young sportsmen are now lost to posterity. Taken c. 1912, it features the 'First XV, St Joseph's College' (The Pines). From a college postcard, the sender was one J. J. Flannery, then only fifteen years of age. It shows a pre-war innocence, and he writes on it to his parents, 'We shall never feel now untill [sic] Xmas so I will say goodbye for a while as I am busy at work'. Young Flannery obviously 'knew his stuff' as he became president of Garbally College in 1947. *(Photo courtesy of Clonfert Diocesan Archive)*

'Loyalty and Courage', the college motto, is also that of the Madden family. The college coat of arms, granted by the Chief Herald in 1959, combines details from the coats of arms of the diocese of Clonfert and the Madden family. Here, the college community is seen in 1927, standing at the front of Garbally House. *(Photo courtesy of Garbally College Archives)*

Senior XV Rugby Team 1929-1930. *(Photo courtesy of Garbally College Archives)*

Fr Peter Greaney, known to students as 'Peader', with *gaelgoirí* in 1929. *(Photo courtesy of Garbally College Archives)*

Junior rugby team, 1924-1925. Seated on the ground, first on the left, is Johnny Howe, a boarder from Derrybrien, who went on to become Bishop Howe of the Columban Order. He served in Burma. The student seated bottom row, far right, is Louis Page, from Woodford. He was president of the college from 1957 to 1963 and died as Monsignor Page in 1999. *(Photo courtesy of Garbally College Archives)*

St Joseph's College, Esker, 1895. Many of these young men became priests – one became a Bishop – the forerunner of The Pines and Garbally. *(Photo courtesy of Garbally College Archives)*

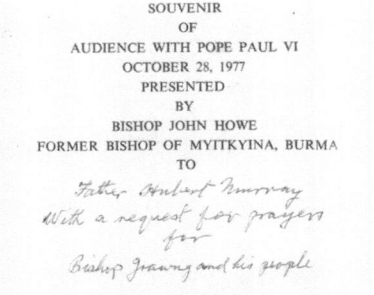
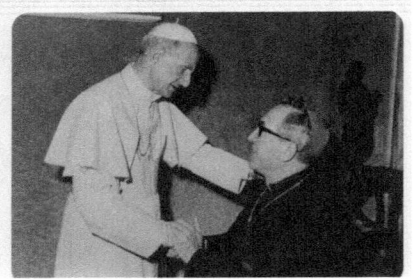

Above left: Henry Byrne from Edenderry, a past pupil who became a Columban Bishop in the Philippines. His brother was Fr Dermot. *(Photo courtesy of Garbally College Archives)*

Above right: Bishop Howe with Pope Paul VI in October 1977. *(Photo courtesy of Clonfert Diocesan Archive)*

1943 – official school photo taken at the base of 'The Obelisk' near the West Lawn. *(Photo courtesy of Garbally College Archives)*

Gymnastics formation, 1924. *(Photo courtesy of Garbally College Archives)*

The 1942 Jubilee – assembled guests reminisce. *(Photo courtesy of Garbally College Archives)*

Above: The 1942 Jubilee – Fr Billy Naughton (holding the homburg) entertains some of his clerical contemporaries. Shortly after this was taken, Fr Billy undertook the perilous sea journey to Los Angeles where he ministered for some years. *(Photo courtesy of Garbally College Archives)*

Left: The 1942 Jubilee – Fr Joseph Cunniffe and Mr Tom O'Meara take note of the photographer while Fr Willie Cummins flicks a cigarette. *(Photo courtesy of Garbally College Archives)*

1942 celebrations – Fr Thomas H. Naughton, Revd Prof. Tom Fahy and Fr Michael O'Connor. Fr Naughton was a native of the town, being born in Attyrory and finishing his days as Parish Priest of Ballymacward. His brother, William, was principal of Creagh national school for many years and resided at Kilgarve House. *(Photo courtesy of Clonfert Diocesan Archive)*

Fr Thomas Dunne (1875-1967) and Fr Peter Greaney (1897-1953) share a joke at the Jubilee celebrations. Dunne, who was a native of Killeenadeema, was a rather laconic individual and was educated at the old diocesan college of St Brendan's and at Esker. He was C.C. of Ballinasloe from 1910 to 1914. Later, as P.P. of Killeenadeema, he had a bomb fired at the door of his residence from a passing police lorry on account of his Republican sentiments. His nephew, Peter, became Catholic Adm. in Ballinasloe in the sixties. Fr Greaney came from Bettaville, Killoran, and was president of Garbally College from 1944 to 1947. He had been educated at The Pines and became a professor of Irish there shortly after his ordination and before the college closed. Loved by all who had the privilege of knowing him, it was only six weeks from the time he first became confused celebrating Mass in the parish of New Inn to the time of his death from an inoperable brain tumour. *(Photo courtesy of Clonfert Diocesan Archive)*

The 1942 Jubilee - less health-conscious days, most of these past pupils are enjoying their cigarettes! The ubiquitous Monsignor Timothy Joyce looks on like a clerical Cheshire cat. *(Photo courtesy of Garbally College Archives)*

Golden Jubilee of the College 1942. Front row (left to right): Prof. M. Tierney, Fr Holohan, Monsignor Joyce, P. Larkin, Dr Surgeon Barniville. Back row: Fr Fallon, Dan Corry, Fr Hughes, Fr Reid, W. O'Rourke and Dr O'Farrell. *(Photo courtesy of Garbally College Archives)*

Jubilee 1942 - Fr Pat Jennings, an t'Áthair Eric MacFhinn, Prof. Martin Murphy and Martin Joyce. *(Photo courtesy of Garbally College Archives)*

Jubilee 1942 - Messrs. Joyce, Cunningham, Murphy. Martin Joyce had a keen interest in local history and carried out much research on the battlefield at Aughrim. *(Photo courtesy of Garbally College Archives)*

A gathering of heavyweights – the official photograph of the 1942 Jubilee celebrations, with past staff and pupils of the Clonfert diocesan colleges. *(Photo courtesy of Garbally College Archives)*

Jubilee celebrations 1942 – an t'Áthair Eric MacFhinn reads an address to Most Revd Dr Dignan (centre), Fr Cogavin (far left) and Prof. Larkin, Prof. Fahy and Prof. Tierney (all past students). *(Photo courtesy of Garbally College Archives)*

Past Pupils' Union meeting in Dublin c. 1960. The P.P.U. was formed by Fr James Cogavin in 1930. *(Photo courtesy of Garbally College Archives)*

The cast of *Iolanthe*, or the *Peer and the Peri* (1930), with the redoubtable Miss Sheridan. *(Photo courtesy of Garbally College Archives)*

College orchestra, 1931, with Lavinia 'Breezy' Sheridan. Holding the cello (first on the left) is a young Patrick Kevin Egan (1911-2001) who later became Very Revd Dr Egan and wrote the seminal local history, *The Parish of Ballinasloe*, in 1959. It was republished in 1994. The cellist (first right) is Vincent Kenny. The violinist (seated first left) is Joe Grenham, whose family owned a grocery shop and a bar on Main Street. Joe went on to manage the business himself. *(Photo courtesy of Clonfert Diocesan Archive)*

'Apple' Annie Delaney who was college matron for many years. *(Photo courtesy of Garbally College Archives)*

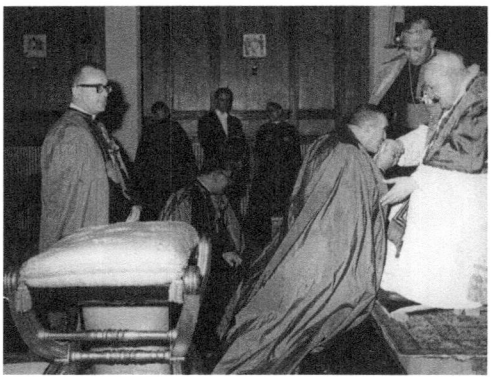

Dr Tom Ryan, Bishop of Clonfert (1964-1983), venerates Blessed Pope John XXIII. Bishop Ryan had been Pope John's secretary. A native of Tipperary, the college sports' complex and the Madden Block were built in his time as patron of the college. *(Photo courtesy of Garbally College Archives)*

Miss 'Breezy' Sheridan, shortly before her retirement from the staff of the college. *(Photo courtesy of Garbally College Archives)*

Michael Hyland who became Garbally's first lay-principal in 1988. He joined the staff in 1957, teaching agricultural science, and was a mainstay of the college until the time of his retirement in 1998. *(Photo courtesy of Garbally College Archives)*

Christmas 1956 - a rugby match in full flow, Garbally Park. *(Photo courtesy of Garbally College Archives)*

Christmas 1956: Two sides compete in a line-out, Garbally Park. *(Photo courtesy of Garbally College Archives)*

Garbally House overlooking the lake, drained since the 1950s. *(Photo courtesy of Garbally College Archives)*

Cast of *Oliver* (1986). Fagin (bearded) is Brian Hayes, T.D., most likely a future Taoiseach. *(Photo courtesy of Garbally College Archives)*

Cast of *Oliver* (1968). *(Photo courtesy of Garbally College Archives)*

Left: Mrs Eileen Quinn, who produced the college operas for many years and was a long-term member of staff. Eileen was also a founding member of the Relays Drama Group. Now retired, she is an accomplished painter. *(Photo courtesy of Garbally College Archives)*

Below: Brian Hayes, T.D., Adrian Kelly and Donal Burke in an offstage scene from *The Maid of the Mountains* (1985). *(Photo courtesy of Fr Declan Kelly, private collection)*

Right: Michael O'Boyle, who looked after Garbally's 'cogs and wheels' for many years. *(Photo courtesy of Garbally College Archives)*

Below left: Mr Joe Finn, a loyal member of the college staff for many years. *(Photo courtesy of Garbally College Archives)*

Below right: Christy Higgins, who was the college farm steward (1924-1971). He lived at the college gate lodge where he and his wife Nonie had a great welcome for all visitors. *(Photo courtesy of Garbally College Archives)*

Above left: Mr John O'Meara, a distinguished past pupil of Garbally and author of *The Singing Masters*. *(Photo courtesy of Garbally College Archives)*

Above right: First-year class of 1965 with staff members Mr Kevin Thornton and Fr John Kirby. *(Photo courtesy of Garbally College Archives)*

HMS Pinafore (1982). Kay Purcell conducts the cast and chorus in the finale. This was the first of the operas Fr (now Bishop) John Kirby revived after becoming college president. The operas had ended in the early seventies after which a number of 'straight' dramatic pieces were presented. *(Photo courtesy of Garbally College Archives)*

Mr Michael Hyland with senior students in 1958. *(Photo courtesy of Garbally College Archives)*

The first transition-year class, 1974-1975, with Mr Michael Hyland and Mr Mike Lally. *(Photo courtesy of Garbally College Archives)*

Above left: Cast of *The Black Stranger* (1980) which focused on the plight of those affected by the potato famine. *(Photo courtesy of Clonfert Diocesan Archive)*

Above right: Bishop Tom Stewart, SSC, a Columban Bishop, who was a past pupil of Garbally. *(Photo courtesy of Garbally College Archives)*

'Ógras' (1970s) with Irish teacher, Mr Gus McNamara. A native of Loughrea, Gus was one of the most popular members of staff in the college until his untimely death in 1999. For some years he also edited the college magazine, *The Fountain*. *(Photo courtesy of Garbally College Archives)*

Deans of discipline with senior members of the Boarders' Council 1975. Back row: Michael Lally (Dean), Peter Quinn, Paul Martin. Front row: Fr Colm Allman (Dean), John Carr. Fr Allman joined the staff in 1971, becoming president in 1990. He was, as one of his predecessors put it at the time, a 'popular appointment'. The tasteful keeping of the college grounds is due to his redoubtable efforts. *(Photo courtesy of Garbally College Archives)*

The earliest production of Gilbert and Sullivan's *The Mikado* (1929). This perennial favourite has been produced by college students no fewer than ten times over the years. As 'Ko-Ko, Lord High Executioner' (sword resting on shoulder) is Tom Kenny from Mountbellew. *(Photo courtesy of Garbally College Archives)*

Junior rugby team 1956-57 with Fr Donal Flanagan. *(Photo courtesy of Garbally College Archives)*

St Joseph's Day 1992. Each year to celebrate the college's patron saint, Joseph the Worker, prizes are awarded to students who excel in academic, social or sporting disciplines. *(Photo courtesy of Garbally College Archives)*

Bishop John Kirby and a former student, Noel Treacy, T.D., outside St Brendan's Cathedral, Loughrea, on the occasion of its centenary in October 2003. Dr Kirby taught at Garbally from 1963 to 1988, when he was appointed Bishop of Clonfert. He was the first native bishop of the diocese since Dr Thomas Coen (1771-1847). *(Photo courtesy of Fr C. Geraghty)*

Staff photo (June 1968). Back row: Fr J. Cassidy, P. Filan, Fr B. Flanagan, Mr M. Hyland, Fr J. Kirby, Mr J. Molloy, Fr V. Marren (RIP), Mr K. Thornton, Fr C. O'Byrne, Mr P. Hession, Fr K. Kitching. Front row: Fr C. Glynn (RIP), Fr J. Higgins, Mr J.C. McGahon (RIP), Mrs E. Quinn, Fr D. Byrne (RIP), J. Ryan, Fr T. Keyes (RIP), Fr K. Ryle (RIP), Fr T. Kennedy (RIP). *(Photo courtesy of Garbally College Archives)*

Above left: C. 1968: Dr Michael Casey (outgoing president, P.P.U.), Dr Donal Burke (incoming president, P.P.U.), Fr Dermot Byrne (college president). *(Photo courtesy of Garbally College Archives)*

Above right: 1990: *The Mikado*... letting the punishment fit the crime. *(Photo courtesy of Garbally College Archives)*

'Three Little Maids from School' (1990). *(Photo courtesy of Garbally College Archives)*

'To the inn we're marching'... *The Student Prince* (1988). *(Photo courtesy of Garbally College Archives)*

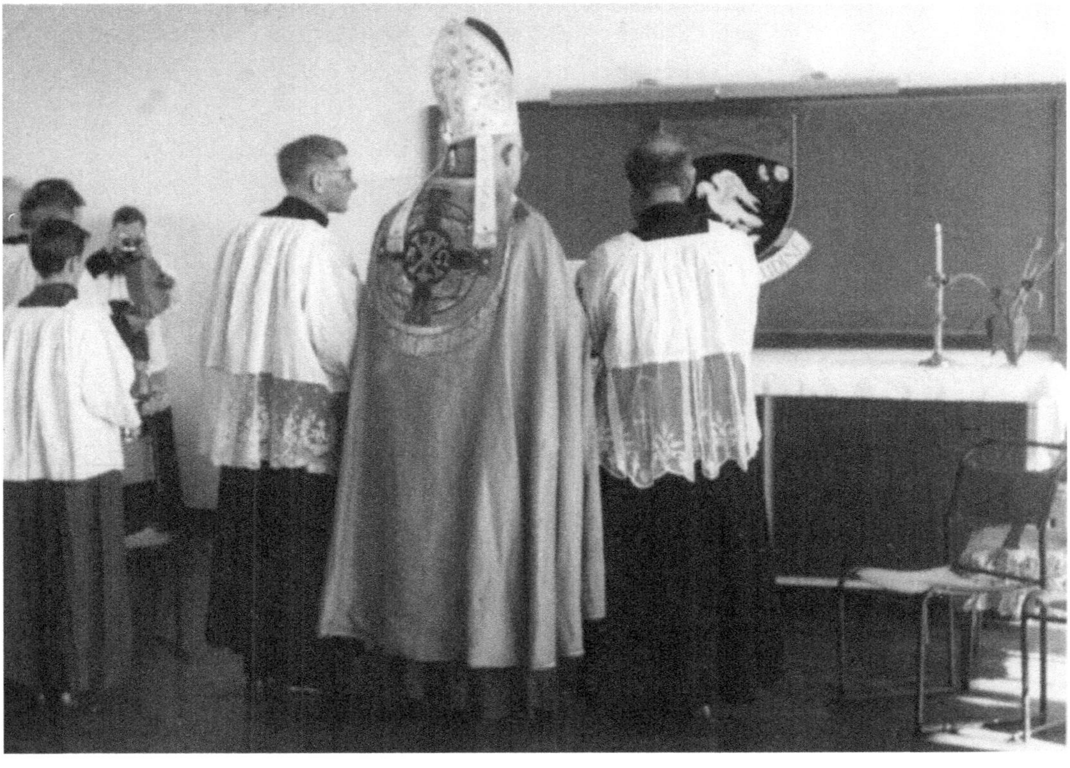

C. 1965 – Bishop Ryan blesses new class halls. *(Photo courtesy of Garbally College Archives)*

Above: Drill display (1933-1934). *(Photo courtesy of Garbally College Archives)*

Left: Monsignor Tom Keyes (1914-1990), president of Garbally College from 1969 to 1973. He guided the school through difficult years in terms of world events. A past pupil himself, in his early years as a professor he was much influenced by Fr Cogavin. He is remembered with great affection by those who were privileged to have known him. *(Photo courtesy of Garbally College Archives)*

three

Folklore, Forgotten Places and People

Old Streets and Residential Areas

Given the upsurge of building in the town in recent years, it may be worthwhile to take some time to reflect on some of the old place names, most of which are now forgotten. Each lane usually derived its name from the surname of the family that first took up residence there or lived at its entrance.

Iver's Lane: Between Garbally Jewellers and Woods, this is the last extant example of the old lane. An interesting remnant of times gone by is the 'Tailor's Bridge' (still visible) which connected Woods to a storeroom. Apparently, a favourite pastime of the tailors employed by Woods on a Saturday afternoon was to loll about on the bridge and watch the more inebriated residents engage in fisticuffs. Like virtually all the other lanes, it became a condemned area and was closed in the early 1940s due to its unsanitary and dangerous condition.

Hopson's Lane: Situated between Grenham's and Cahalan's Jewellers, up until only recently it contained the shell of 'Mommie' Higgins' house. The daughter of a blacksmith and one of the last washerwomen in Ballinasloe, 'Mommie', was a great character who apparently had a 'cure' for eye complaints. She would pluck a thorn from a bush and, holding it perilously close to the sufferer's eye, would rotate it while reciting the 'Hail Mary'. It was never known to fail! She had a narrow brush with death in the 1940s when her house was struck by lightning, blasting in the front window.

Tea (Pronounced 'Tae') Lane: Now Jubilee Street, it is the best known of the old lanes. It derived its name from a number of three- or four-storey warehouses where tea, brought down the canal, was stored. These warehouses, when demolished, were replaced by one-storey dwellings. The name was changed in 1923 at the suggestion of the local clergy who wished to commemorate the occasion of the Jubilee of the Holy Family Confraternity.

Woodslip Lane: Located beside Keller's, it derived its name from the slips of wood made there by resident coopers for the barrels supplied to Brewery Yard. It closed in the 1930s when the final remaining residents were forcibly evicted. As a consequence, one elderly lady and former resident, while inebriated, was often heard to denounce the local TD by bawling, 'Up Dev, but to hell with Paddy Beegan!'

Paradise Row: A lane of small houses, the entrance to which once stood where the post office is now located. Even though it ran parallel to the Market Square, it was obscured behind other houses which faced onto the Square. Abandoned by its residents in the early 1930s, it contained barely habitable dwellings even at the height of its occupancy and thus 'Paradise Row' was a derisory and ironic name.

Boulger's Lane: Formerly between Hill's and Duane's old chemist shop, it is probably one of the oldest of all the lanes and closed only in the 1950s. This was where Denny Delaney, the famous blind piper, lived. His contribution to music and to the town is commemorated on a plaque at the entrance to the lane. This entrance also contains an interesting arch stone bearing the date 1783.

Waterloo Place: This was to be found at the rear of St Gabriel's Convent of Mercy and derived its name from the number of families residing there whose fathers or husbands were veterans of the Napoleonic Wars. It was also the site of a military barracks.

The Kennels: Built in 1949 and now known as St Michael's Place, the area derived its name from the hounds kept there by a local hunt. It was also known as Newtowngaffy. In 1865, there were nearly one hundred residents living there.

Agricultural Lane: Beside the town hall, this lane received its name from its close proximity to the Agricultural Hall. Later called 'The Plaza', it is now known as Emmet Place.

Although little is known regarding some of the streets and residential areas, they are mentioned below in order to give a more comprehensive picture of the town.

Reeve's Lane: Beside the Dunlo Tavern, this is now known as Davitt Place.

Well Lane: Off Jubilee Street and opposite Reeve's Lane, it only ever held a few families.

Victoria Street: This is now Duggan Avenue, to commemorate Bishop Patrick Duggan of Clonfert.

Brewery Yard: Behind Egan's Pub in Main Street, this was a residential area and was once the location of a brewery.

The Glebe: Situated on Dunlo Hill (now a park area), it was formerly home to clusters of stunted furze trees.

Piper's and Rutledge's Lane: Both are now completely demolished but stood at the entrance to the present Hymany Park.

Though the 'lanes' were occupied by respectable families, one of the most insulting

names that could be attached to a person in Ballinasloe was that of 'a laner'.
In the 1930s, an t'Áthair Eric McFhinn (1895-1987) travelled about recording the recollections of older residents of the twenty-four parishes in Clonfert diocese. He was complimented in that regard by Revd Dr P. K. Egan, who, over the course of his twenty-two-year ministry in the town, gathered a vast amount of information from parishioners. Without that work most of the folklore in the diocesan archives would not now exist. Included here are some of the recollections gathered by an t'Áthair Eric and Dr Kevin.

Mrs Carroll, Perssepark:

> The station at St Grellan's Well began on September 19th and continued until October 5th. You begin your station around the hill seven times, say one 'Our Father', one 'Hail Mary' and one 'Gloria' each time, then go around the well fifteen times and say one 'Our Father', one 'Hail Mary' and one 'Gloria'. Each turn, always start your station to your left. When you finish, say three 'Our Fathers', three 'Hail Marys' and three 'Glorias' in honour of St Grellan and take three drinks of water out of the well.

Joseph Shaughnessy, Glantane, Ballinasloe:

> Jack Donelan, now sixty-five years of age.
> Famous athlete.
> Ran for Ireland in England in ten-mile cross-country race, being first man home for Ireland.
> Won fifty-mile handicap races.
> Connaught champion for a number of years.
> Won the six-mile cross-country championship for Ireland four times: twice junior and twice senior and several two- and four-mile races as well.

Mrs Ryan, Parkmore, Ballinasloe:

> The marriages in olden times were quite different to the present-day marriages. They [sic] older people were very superstitious. They would not let a couple get married on odd days. They would count from Christmas Day and that day was the even day. It was unlucky to marry in the month of May. The bride would wear something blue and something old. In olden times, they had big weddings. Two or three barrels of porter and a big dinner of bacon and cabbage and potatoes. It was not a lucky marriage if the strawboys did not come. Before the marriage, there was the matchmaking and the fortune had to be given to the man and some kept back for the next year. The bride was shy and would not go to Mass for the first Sunday until the following Sunday. Then, she would have what they called a 'show-off' – that was all the new relatives would have new hats which were bought by the new married couple. The bride would not go home for a month. Nowadays, all this custom is done away with. Boys and girls make their own matches.

Mr Murray, Ballyhugh:

> On a little hill near the Athlone road in the village of Birchgrove, a man was hanged in Fenian times… this man went out at night gathering money. This was not right, so he was caught and tried in court and hanged from a bush on the hill.

Bridie Kelleher, Creagh:

> Marriages that take place in the month of May are supposed to be unlucky. Also on Monday and Friday in the week.

Cures

Mrs Naughton, Attycorry, cure for a chin cough:

> Some people used to feed ferrets with bread and milk and whatever they would refuse to eat they would put it in a cup and take it to the sick child and make the child eat it all so after three days it would be better.

Mr Murray, Ballyhugh:

> Perhaps one of the best cures for the chin cough was to get a saucer of meal and bring it to an ass, let the ass breathe on it. Then boil it and give it to the child and in a few days the child would be cured.

Ointment

> The ointment commonly used for ringworm or on any other scabs was tar and bluestone mixed together. This was called 'green plaster'.

Mrs Cunningham, Market Square, Ballinasloe, cure for a sore throat:

> …to put coarse salt down in the pan until it gets hot. Then take it up and put it into a woolen sock and put it around your neck.

Prayers

Mrs Naughton, Attyrory, prayer going to bed:

> I own Good Friday, I own Good Friday. It was on Good Friday our Saviour was crucified. They plaited a crown of thorns. They perched them on His head. They came with their spears so sharp and they pierced our Saviour through the breast. Whoever says this prayer by night or day, neither death nor danger nor the gates of hell shall they ever enter.

Mrs Kelleher, Dunlo Street, Ballinasloe, a night prayer:

> May the will of God be done by us,
> May the death of the saints be won by us
> and the light of the Kingdom begun in us;
> May Jesus the child be beside my bed,
> May the Lamb of Mercy uplift my head,
> May the Virgin Mary her brightness
> Shed and Michael the steward of my soul.

Mrs Hanniffy, Creagh, a night prayer:

> Jesus, be with me this night, every stir and move I do, that I may do so in honour of you, Jesus. All for thee, my Jesus, sweet Jesus, it is you I do adore.
> Holy Blessed Virgin, intercede to Jesus for me and keep me in sanctity and purity all the days of my life, for Jesus sake. Amen.

Seán Ryan, Creagh:

> Jesus the branch and Mary the flower,
> Jesus and Mary be with me in my dying hour.

Miscellaneous

John Naughton, Attycorry, Creagh – Creagh Graveyard:

> 'The south ruin' is supposed to be knocked by Cromwell or some of his followers. The new graveyard, i.e. the middle portion, 'was opened in the year 1885 and the first remains that were buried in it was a woman called Bridget Davis and was interred on September 3rd, 1885.'
>
> 'The late Matt Harris, MP, from East Galway is buried here. The monument erected over him is one of the best there and was erected by his fellow countrymen as a tribute to his patriotism. This particular stone was erected by Mr Beegan.'

Pisreoga

J. Hanniffy, Creagh:

> Old people believed that if a man had a coal in his pipe, they would not let him out for fear the butter would go along with him. They also believed that fairies could steal the butter and to prevent this, they used to put a red coal under the churn or leave the new tongs near it. If you went out early to the field where your neighbours' cows are grazing and perform certain things, the butter would follow you home.

Brendan Ryan, Parkmore:

> When a new milk cow is bought, they burn the hair of the udder with a candle and then brush it. They also tie ribbons on her tail.

Annie Cogavin, Suckfield, lucky days:

> People say that Friday is the luckiest. Wednesday is said to be a day for a cure. All people go ploughing on a Friday and also, when they are changing into a new house, Friday is the lucky day. When the moon is on the go back, it is the best time to sow cabbage where it won't go to seed. It is said that April borrowed three days from May to kill the old cow. Queen Elizabeth said on Michaelism [sic] night was the first goose she ate on the 1st of September.

Bridie Kelleher, Creagh:

> If you turn your churn towards the door on a May morning before the sun comes out and say these words 'butter, butter, come' and you will get all your neighbours' butter to follow you.
>
> The lucky day in my district is Friday. The unlucky day is Tuesday. People change on Friday. The day on which cures are given is Friday. The worst day of the year in my district is known as Whit Monday because if you go near water on that day, you will get drowned. People never spend money on that day, because you will be spending it all the year.

Bridie Kelleher, Dunlo Street, houses in former times:

> The houses in former times were made of mud and very small doors and they were thatched. The thatch is got from the oats. The old homes had a bed in the kitchen. The bed was used for a chair in the evening and a bed at night. The name of it was a settled bed. The fireplace was always placed in the gable. The fireplace was never placed in the corner or against the sidewall. The old chimneys were made with rods and plastered with cow dung and whitewashed over that. In the Penal days, the people used to light a fire in the centre of the floor and put a hole in the roof. There were some houses with no glass and, at night, there was a bag put up in place of the glass. The old floors were made of earth or clay. Half-doors are not common now. Long ago, people used to use turf for their fires. They used to have rushes dipped in grease for light at night. Candles were not made locally.

Anthony McDonnell, Creagh:

> The fireplace was mostly always placed in the gable. The chimneys were made very queer. They had a big plank across the house and a rod chimney built and plastered with clay. Mortar floors were made of sand and lime… in olden times they used dipped rushes and candles. All the candles were made locally. The days which cure ailments are as follows: on the 21 of June patterning of Taughmaconnell, the 13th of July the patterning of Brideswell.
>
> In years gone by, they used to plough with a wooden plough but it is not done now. The old roads that are still used are Parkmore, Ruane and the Newline. The rate of pay was meal. The bridge was not always over the Suck. They were only built in 1887.

Ignatius Hanniffy, Creagh, hauling home:

> Long ago when marriages took place, customs which are now done away with always were used. The bride used to go to her father's home not to her husbands. As she is entering the house, one of the women breaks an oaten cake on her head. She stays in that house for a spell of about a month. Then, at about dusk on a Friday, she is accompanied by her friends in sidecars. She would take with her some presents from her mother such as linen, blue cap and an old purse. Bonfires are lit and also torches of flames. It consists of a sod soaked in paraffin oil and tar on top of a hay fork.

Sean Ryan, Creagh:

Years ago, crosses were made with oaten straw with the grain on the crosses. These were stuck into the houses on St Brigid's night. The crosses are nearly always made by the head of the house. When the farmer is about to sow the oats in the spring, he takes down the cross and removes the grain. He shakes holy water on it. This is the first seed he sows.

Jackie Ward, Creagh N.S., hauling home:

On a Friday evening just before dusk, the bride would get her sidecar and she would bring plenty of linen. Her carpenter would make a box with a lock and a key. In this box she would keep her linen and other things her mother would give her. When she would come near her husband's house, people would put bone [sic] fires on hills… that night they would have a dance. During that time they would get an outer door and they would put it on the floor. Then the best dancers would dance jigs, reels and hornpipes.

Killbegley Hill is so-called because once there was a priest murdered by a man named Begley. Police used to be looking for him so the people used to say 'kill Begley'.

Jas. White, town clerk:

The old mail-coach road crossed the Suck at a ford in front of St Michael's church and reached the present road at Mark Killallea's. At the bend in the river near the present ash pit below St Michael's was a deep spot called 'Pull-a-Thúfhal'.

Jas. White, town clerk:

The old road went down by Finn's in Creagh and out at Birchgrove, passing slightly to the south of present road and skirting Birchgrove Gardens.

Pat Carney, N.T.:

There is a townland of the name 'Cloynigne' near Killure church with an old castle in it.

Pat Molloy, N.T.:

A very old road passed across Mount Pleasant, through Garbally and joined the present road near Knocknagreena. There still remains the ruins of a public house which was on it just back of the present technical school in O'Flynn's field. Presumably it came out at Dunlo Hill.

Revd Eamon Dooley, Dalgan Park (1947):

The new line from Cuileen to Creagh was built about 1881. The stones from Admiral St George's home in Sallaville were used.

A very large wood existed from Finnerans of Cuileen to Donoghues of Castlepark as late as… 1915. Timber sold to Flanagan's saw mills.

The nunnery ruins were cleared… in land reclamation. Some mounds still remain.

Miscellaneous snippets:

St Michael's Square was once an orchard.

The mailcoach yard was at Woods – the high archway.

There was a brewery at the back of Tower View, Flanagan's – after the soldiers left.

There was a Tannery at the back o' the old barracks in River Street. The holes are there still – Mocler's Tanyard.

The Ribbonmen they were in my father's time. They'd pull you out of bed to join them. A lot of young men that wouldn't join them went away – nearly all to Liverpool – an' came back when the times were quiet.

He found it in a wall of Clontuskert Abbey. About priests to be in Garbally was in it. (About 'Cunningham's Prophecy')

The Dowager Clancarty was something to Ormonde.

The schools of Clancarty were there since the time of the Famine – lots of Catholics used to go – on Dunlo Hill – they'd get dinner.

All Derrymullen went to the school.

About sixty years ago there were a lot of Irish teachers about places – night teachers. Fellows working would go at night, give two pence a night and bring turf. The teachers were Roger MacSwiney and Rigney. I remember one in the lane.

All ould people in town, about sixty years ago, knew Irish, a lot in from the country.

'Pounds of bacon leases' – workers got a lease in Garbally on condition of eating a pound of bacon on Friday.

The Divil visited Lancaster. Ould Lancaster was a terrible gambler. 'If I had anyone to play cards,' he said, 'even if it was the Divil himself'. A stranger came. It was the middle of the night before he came. The minister then could not hunt him. The priest, Father Lorcan, hunted him – through the wall. The ould wan said one devil could hunt another. Someone said Father Lorcan should put him back. He said he had too much trouble hunting him.

Author's Note

(A later version of this story has Fr John P. Heenan in it, playing cards in the Freemason's Lodge which stood at Lower Main Street.)

The Archdeacon's Monument was going to be built in the green. But Daniel O'Connell stopped it, brought it before Parliament.

The Archdeacon's bush is at the Red Bridge – the first bridge from the railway – he used to preach there.

(These snippets were recorded from Katie Quigley. At one time, a Katie Quigley who was a professional photographer had a studio in Duggan Avenue. Whether or not this is the same lady who was interviewed by Fr MacFhinn is unknown to me.)

I heard my mother say that a priest – an uncle of ould George Philipps – Father O'Connor, P.P. in New Inn – he was comen home from a sick call early on May mornen, at the break of day. (Everybody in the country locks up the cows on May mornen.) An this one was waven her charm or her spell an she was sayen, 'All to me, all to me'. 'Ah, then, half to me,' says he – just somethen to say – a day or two after, when his housekeeper was churnen the milk, she couldn't stir the churndash hardly, there was too much butter. She got frightened an she called him. He was thinken awhile, an he thought o' the ould one. So he said to get a bottle an filled it with milk an put it on the fire. Accorden as twas getten hot, she came cryen to the door – oh, screamen. How well she knew where to come – I suppose somethen dragged her. He made her go on her knees an promise that she'd give everyone back their butter.

The charms is from the druids.
Colonel Thornhill's butter was taken he was at Killgarv [sic].
Butter was taken at Taughmaconnell. The friars were brought.

The Rocks

Miss Rock was the last. John Rock was, I think, her father's name. All are buried in Creagh. They had a sort of little vault. The headstone is to the left, to one side, near where Miss Tully is buried. They had a hotel where, Glennon, the teacherman, is, next Kelly's Hotel, which was not there that time. She died in Dublin. Her funeral came down here. She died before I remember.

* The soldiers at Garbally saw the Archdeacon on the Broad Walk.

Creagh church was said by Dr Healy to have been built by St Patrick.

On St Grellan's Day the old people used to go to the well. Fr Joyce brought them once, but to Kilclooney church, not to the right place. Kilclooney church is said never to have been consecrated. It was said to have been made in the night time. The Catholics built it. The building was stopped. Anyone who steals a stone is haunted. The water is said not to boil.

*Author's Note

The 'soldiers' referred to were those billeted at the house during the 'Troubles'. This is obviously a local ghost story of the time. In local lore, Garbally has been the focal point of many supernatural tales. A former long-term member of college staff, the late Christy Higgins, often recalled how as a young farm steward he once saw 'a white lady' sitting on a rock in the middle of the old lake (long-since drained). She was combing her hair with a large white comb. Christy informed Fr Cogavin who performed a special blessing there. Long before, the lake had claimed the life of a butler who had been skating there and fell through the ice.

Ghost stories from around the town take on an apocryphal form, though one incident in particular, which allegedly happened in 1916, stands out. A large, luminous 'flying object' hovered over the town for about five hours. While ufologists would have a field day with such an event, the truth of the matter, if indeed any exists, is probably that an airship of some description strayed over the town's airspace. One seriously doubts that passing Martians took an interest in buying horses at the fair!

'Bishop Coen lived where Flanagan's Mills are now – it was an old barracks for Germans – mercenaries. They drowned themselves in *Poll a Tuafail* – there is a whirlwind in it – a queer thing pulls them down. It is called the German's Hole. Sea serpents are said to be there, in a cave under the ivy castle. Lord Clancarty sacked the man who would not go down for the second German.'

Bernie Mulkerns (1948):
'A priest was shot at the well of St Grellan while saying Mass. When falling, he left his hand on a stone cross there and the imprint remains. Clancarty closed the well, but had to re-open it due to some misfortune that befell him. He then had it walled-in and steps put down to it'.

Author's Note

(A similar story concerns a holy well in the parish of Mullagh/Killoran, some considerable distance from Ballinasloe. While I have no documentary evidence for this, only two years ago a man taking photos of this site for me claimed to have experienced great difficulty in doing so, as if, he said, someone were continuously placing a hand across the lens of the camera.)

John Horne (Moher, 1948):
'Fr Larkin (Archdeacon Lorcan) went round the parish and had all the Bibles, which were distributed by the Protestants, collected with a donkey and cart and burned them on the canal bank, for which he was prosecuted.'

(Written references to the Archdeacon give his name variously as 'Larkin', 'Lorcan', and, in Wolfe Tone's memoirs, as 'Larking'. Tone, one suspects, was being facetious. Archdeacon Lorcan was P.P. of Ballinasloe from 1792 to 1825).

John Holloway: 'A man called Don Brien who had one hand had a hedge school.'

Andy Staunton: '"The Pines" as a Protestant college was closed before 1890'. He saw old books and bibles in Irish there. He heard that there was a similar college in Fortwilliam.

A Dolly Murray had a hedge school in Cuileen about 1860. She had some kind of disability. The pupils brought turf for the fire and made payments towards her support.

Rory Kilduff

We live in an age of contradictions. Half the world is fighting the 'battle of the bulge' to lose weight, while the other half tries to stave off starvation just to stay alive. Technology has sent men to the moon, yet next-door neighbours often don't know each others' names. In such a society it is refreshing to find bedrock, and one such certainty is Rory Kilduff. At eighty-five years of age it is no wonder he has a great sense of history.

Born in the same week that Michael Collins was shot, he is one of the last surviving old harness-makers. He came into the business, however, quite by accident. His father, Rody, who was a native of Clonfad, became apprenticed to the business on Main Street in 1880, with a man called Charlie Greaney. Rody finally took over the business in 1916. Being the equivalent in its day of the modern garage, it employed nine men at one point. Rory came on board when his father got a heart attack in 1937, and he worked until his retirement in 1997.

Some local events are especially prominent in his memory, such as the 1932 Congress. At the time, there were only about three wirelesses in Ballinasloe and a number of old crystal sets. One of the wealthiest business families of the time were the Conroys, whose business was located where the present NIB now stands. Rincie Conroy (who went on to become a judge) put the wireless in the window for some three hundred people to hear the final proceedings of the Congress, as they recited the rosary.

He also recalls the collapse of Beckett's Pub in 1947. At the time, Rory was on his way to the railway station to collect a parcel. On his way there, the pub was still standing, but on his way back it had fallen! Fortunately, the workmen were on their dinner break. However, the Flanagan family were not so lucky when the same fate befell their home in 1896 at the top left-hand corner of Market Square. Husband and wife were both killed and a son, Tom, was orphaned. He later became a reporter for *The Freeman's Journal*.

He remembers the characters of the town vividly, such as the now long-dead bank manager who had a penchant for spinning tall yarns. This same gentleman claimed to have served on board a battleship in the First World War and to have spent three weeks drinking in Leenane with Winston Churchill!

He has seen many families come and go, such as the Lancasters, once quite prominent businesspeople who originally came from Wicklow. He remembers the ancient Forester's Hall burning down in 1940 and the Working Mans' Club moving to 'The Hut' on the Fair Green.

There are no harness-makers left in Ireland now, one of the last surviving, Sam Greer from Dublin, dying recently. Yet, Rory Kilduff does not pine for the 'old days' nor does he seek refuge in them. Living happily in retirement with Maura, his wife for over fifty years, Rory can be seen sallying forth daily from his home on Main Street to chat with both young and old. He remains as much a certainty in Ballinasloe as the Trench monument or St Michael's Square. He is excellent company and impossible to dislike.

Above: Emmet Browne and Patrick Ward share a joke outside Tim Killeen's old garage on Dunlo Street, c. 1970. *(Photo courtesy of Geraldine Ward)*

Right: Michael Ryan, outside his pub on Society Street, c. 1960s. *(Photo courtesy of Martin Ryan)*

Vintners outing c. 1960. *(Photo courtesy of Martin Ryan)*

St Grellan's boys' school c. 1960. *(Photo courtesy of Clonfert Diocesan Archive)*

Staff at Dubarry Shoe Factory c. 1960s. *(Photo courtesy of F. Walsh)*

The 'Portiuncula Hospital' had its origins in Old Mount Pleasant. It was founded in 1942 by the Franciscan Missionaries of the Divine Motherhood who were invited to the diocese by Bishop John Dignan. The first patient was admitted on 11 February 1943; the first baby was born on 20 February 1943. *(Photo courtesy of FMDM Archives)*

A scene from a summer's day in 1953 outside Rafter's grocery shop (now the ACC Bank) on Main Street, featuring two of the most popular detergents of that time, 'Vim' and 'Rinso'. *(Photo courtesy of Barry Lally)*

Above: Ivan Rafter and family outside his store on Main Street, c. 1970s. Rafters was a highly respected business in Ballinasloe. Far removed from present-day supermarkets, Ivan Rafter was one of the many friendly faces of business in town, who always recognised the dignity of his customers and treated them fairly and decently. *(Photo courtesy of Davey Rafter)*

Left: Another of Ballinasloe's prominent business families was the Croffys. Left is Fr Martin Croffy (1903-1986), who studied at The Pines and became one of the first of its students to join the Maynooth Mission to China or the Columban Order. He was one of the heroic pioneers of the order and, in *The Red Lacquered Gate*, author William E. Barrett related an incident from 1939, 'On April 8, an echo from of old, worrisome days was sounded in Han Yang when bandits invaded Chang Tan Kow and brutally beat Fathers Timothy Leahy and Martin Croffy, who were both hospitalised'. Fr Croffy ended his days more peacefully at Silver Creek in Omaha, Nebraska, where he is buried, although he was a frequent visitor to his hometown. *(Photo courtesy of Catherine Croffy)*

July 1961 – the family gather for Malachy and Maura's 25th wedding anniversary (Maura is seated first on right). Maura Croffy made an outstanding contribution to civic life. A native of Ahascragh, she had been greatly influenced by Archdeacon Malachy Brennan, P.P., who was a champion of the Irish language. She was the first woman to be elected to the Urban District Council, holding her seat for twenty-five years. Later, she won a seat on Galway County Council and was one of the first members of the Western Health Board when it was established. After her death in 1987, a journalist wrote in the *Connacht Tribune*, 'While her profile in public life was always high, there was another side to Maura Croffy. She was, first and last, a good wife and mother…' *(Photo courtesy of Catherine Croffy)*

Hubert Croffy (1943-2006). *(Photo courtesy of Catherine Croffy)*

Passing cyclists on Main Street are caught unawares in this scene c. 1955. The owner of the donkey tethered to the pole is doubtless enjoying a big, creamy pint, while down the avenue can be seen the remains of Woodslip Lane. To the left is 'Cogavin's Hardware Store and China Hall'. *(Photo courtesy of B. Lally)*

Locals and visitors inspect fruit and produce in the Fair Green during the October fair, c. 1935. The only person to be identified here is the clergyman, Fr John Doyle, C.C. *(Photo courtesy of Gerry Stronge)*

Creagh Guild, of the Irish Countrywomen's Association, at a meal in Hayden's Hotel c. 1965. *(Photo courtesy of Creagh I.C.A.)*

Michael Kiely (1896-1970), who had a tailoring and drapery business on Society Street, pictured outside his shop in 1964 in a Local Defence uniform. A native of Limerick, he began his business in the town c. 1930, making the navy-serge uniforms worn by the male nurses in St Brigid's Psychiatric Hospital. Kiely's shop was previously Mag Walshe's Public House. Also featured is Society Fruit Stores, owned by the McCullagh's, who were prominent businesspeople in the town. *(Photo courtesy of Marion Bushell)*

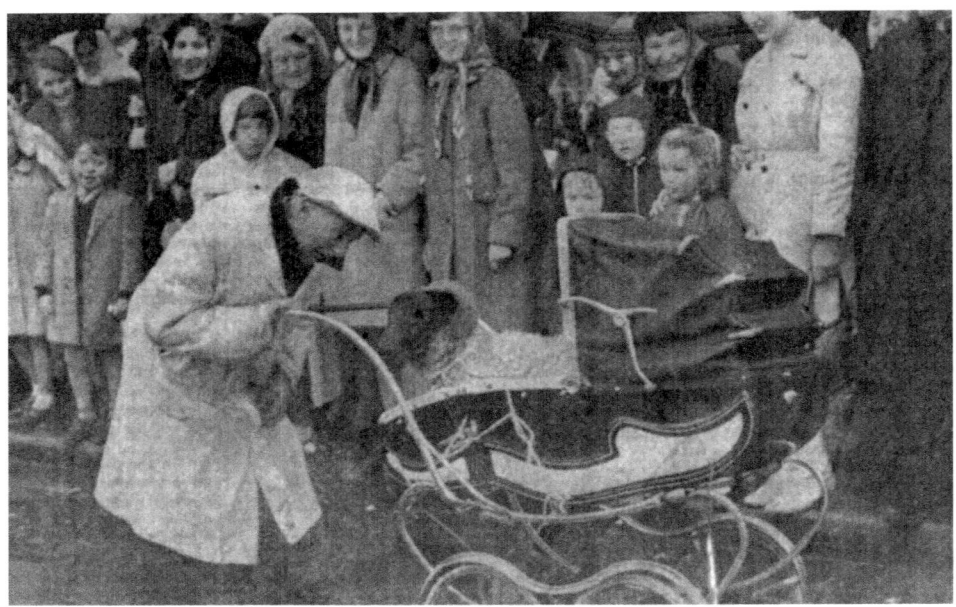

'There was a wild and lonely boy, "Star" Healy was his name…' *(Photo courtesy of Noel Ryan)*

Mick Rankin (1899-1973) who worked for the Grand Canal delivery service from 1930 until 1965. His father, Frank, was a coach driver for Lord Mahon of Castlegar, Ahascragh, and converted from Presbyterianism to Catholicism after marrying his wife. Michael Rankin was the first to deliver by 'motor-lorry' after the cessation of the old cart-horse float. The Canal first opened in 1828 and was a great source of trade and commerce for the town. In 1959, canal traffic ceased, with C.I.E. taking over transport of goods. *(Photo courtesy of Carmel Rankin)*

'Ould Stock…': Jack Fallon, Johnny 'the Gurk' Kelly, Eddie Fallon and Nancy Kelly. All gentlemen came from Derrymullen, Johnny moving to Galway city as a young man. His father had been a blacksmith, John Kelly, from Kilmalaw. Jack Fallon was a well-known 'Eggler', spending his life in the egg and wool trade on Society Street. In the fifties, he bought out the Mannings, who owned the stores. His father had worked for Ambrose Manning, another prominent businessman. Eddie fought in the 1916 Rising, losing a leg in the fight for Irish freedom. Most of the Fallons are buried in Kilclooney cemetery. *(Photo courtesy of Johnny Kelly, Galway)*

Above left: Tom Madden who was a coachman for the last of the Earls of Clancarty. *(Photo courtesy of Phil Bruce)*

Above right: Overview of part of the Fair Green, dotted with sheep, and the glebe. In the background is the spire of St Michael's Church. *(Photo courtesy of Clonfert Diocesan Archive)*

Above and below: Seen outside his bicycle and radio shop on Dunlo Street is Pakie Clarke. He is standing alongside mechanic Jimmy Dunwoody, and Pakie's son, Stanley, who took over the business from his late father. Today, it is still a thriving hardware/bicycle and machine shop. Prior to Pakie Clarke's tenure, it was a drapery store. *(Photo courtesy of Stanley and Margaret Clarke)*

Above left: The Nicholsons who owned a drapery business on Main Street where Woods is now located. Left to right are: Tommy (1890-1941), Reg (1893-1957), Cissie (1897-?), Michael (1881-1955), Molly (1884-1969), Jack (1888-1951), Nan (1891-1948), Martin (1882-1939), Lil (1894-1973), Dee (1885-1952). Seated: Thomas (1837-1926), _____ , Margaret (1856-1917). Michael and Tommy were partners in John Wood & Co., Main Street. Tommy married Josephine McHugh of Rathmines in 1935. Michael, on retirement, went to his sisters at Colwyn Bay, N. Wales. Michael, Tommy and Jack are buried in Creagh cemetery.

Nan went to England and began a nursing home in Colwyn Bay in the late twenties. She was later joined by Dee, Lil and Peg. Lil and Peg later opened a fancy-goods store there. All are buried in Colwyn Bay, as is Molly who also retired there. Jack and Molly worked at Clery's Department Store in Dublin for many years. Paddy and Cissie emigrated to New York; Paddy working as a departmental manager at Reeve's Department Store and marrying a Miss Coffey from Ballinasloe.

Martin fought with the British Army in the Boer War, returning to Ireland in 1915. He moved to Perth, Scotland.

Thomas worked for a number of years as a hotel steward in Hayden's Hotel on Dunlo Street. *(Photo courtesy of Les Nicholson)*

Above right: A rare photograph of Dr Patrick Duggan, Bishop of Clonfert, (1871-1896). In 1933, the main sports field in Ballinasloe, adjacent to Harris Road, was named after him and, in the late forties, when the Gaelic League were renaming the town's streets, Victoria Street became Duggan Avenue.

A native of Cummer, Tuam, he was a noted patriot and was revered by both priests and his people. He had a fierce empathy for their lot as he had witnessed first-hand, as a young priest, the horrors of the Great Famine. The unbalanced Judge William Keogh presided over a trial in 1872, in which Dr Duggan, among many of his own priests, was accused of using undue influence over voters in an election. Though acquitted, Dr Duggan never fully recovered from the experience. He is buried in Glasnevin cemetery.

Though a loyal churchman, he exercised independence in running Clonfert. On one occasion, while hosting a dinner for some noted patriots, he received Leo XIII's rescript condemning the Land League. Having read it, he turned to a servant and said nonchalantly, 'Mike, kill another pig!' *(Photo courtesy of Clonfert Diocesan Archive)*

This scene would possibly be more akin to a film with Messrs. Karloff or Price! Taken in Brennan's Yard, on Main Street (which once stood at the back of where Supermacs is now located), John Lillis is shown atop the old horse-drawn hearse. A lugubrious, but common, feature of town life, such modes of final transport have long since been replaced by the motorised hearse.

John's brother, Mick, was one of the best-known undertakers in the town. Mick lived in the area of Society Street known as 'The Plaza' or 'Emmet Place'. *(Photo courtesy of Kim Lillis)*

Fr John Kelly and an unidentified clergyman (alighting the carriage) are escorted by John Lillis to a day's coursing in Loughrea. *(Photo courtesy of Kim Lillis)*

Right: Andrew Staunton who ran a grocery shop in Creagh. One of the many community-minded citizens of the town, he was a founding member of the Credit Union, the Creagh Community Council and a member of the St Vincent de Paul and the Ballinasloe Choral Society.

A lover of music, he was on friendly terms with RTÉ's Tommy O'Brien and had a vast music collection. Despite being seriously ill, he was working on behalf of the local Lions' Club just shortly before his death. *(Photo courtesy of Marie Staunton)*

Below: A disembodied Joe Higgins as Santa Claus, handing out Christmas surprises to staff in Dubarry. *(Photo courtesy of Phil Bruce)*

Galway footballers, 1925. Standing, from left: Father Ned Hughes, Leonard McGrath, Frank Benson, Sonny Burke, Mick Brennan, Bartley Murray, Paddy Ganley, John Egan, Gilbey Jennings, Jack Deeley, Larry Raftery, Jack Fry, Tom McGrath and Jackie Brennan. Middle row: Mick Bannerton, Mick Donnellan, Tom ('Trixie') Leetch, Tom Molloy (captain); Frank Walsh, Willie Smith and Denis Egan. Front row: Harry Burke, Michael ('Knacker') Walshe (vice-captain), and Paddy Roche.

Ballinasloe played a major role in Galway's first All-Ireland Senior Football victory. The first of Galway's nine All-Ireland Senior Football Championship titles was won in 1925, in controversial, even bizarre circumstances, but there was no doubting its validity or merit.

At that time, the Galway team selection was dominated by the all-conquering Ballinasloe club who were unbeaten in the County Senior Championship from 1913 to 1929, although it should be pointed out, for the record, that the championship was not completed in 1920, '21, '24, '26 and '27. Galway had lost the 1919 All-Ireland final to Kildare and the 1922 final to Dublin. In 1925, the Connacht championship was only at the first-round stage by the time Kerry, Wexford and Cavan had qualified from their respective provincial campaigns, so Mayo were nominated to represent Connacht. In the All-Ireland semi-finals, Kerry defeated Cavan and Mayo defeated Wexford, but after an objection by Cavan and counter-objection by Kerry, both of those counties were disqualified and Mayo were declared champions. However, the Connacht final was then played, with Galway defeating Mayo at Parkmore, Tuam, by 1-5 to 1-3. The Central Council of the G.A.A. then declared Galway the All-Ireland champions. And in a special provincial winners' tournament, run in January 1926, Galway defeated Cavan in the final by 3-2 to 1-2, after earlier eliminating Wexford; Kerry refused to participate. Galway were now All-Ireland champions a second time in the one season, and they received two sets of medals to prove it!

Fortunately, an earlier dispute which threatened Galway's participation in the delayed provincial final was resolved: Ballinasloe's Great October Fair clashed with the date of the match in Tuam between Galway and Mayo (18 October); the Connacht GAA Council turned down a request for a postponement, and it took three special meetings in the town of Ballinasloe to persuade the players to swap the fair weekend for the Connacht final.

The official photograph of the 1925 Galway team shows that the players were all Ballinasloe men except Mick Bannerton (Mountbellew), Harry Burke (Moylough), Mick Donnellan (Dunmore) and Tom Molloy (Corofin). At least one of the quartet (Molloy) played his club football with Ballinasloe and one or two of the others may also have done so. *(Photo courtesy of Jim Kearney)*

'Tommo' and Gertie Madden, Brackernagh, parents of Fr P.J. *(Photo courtesy of Madden Family)*

Fr P.J. Madden who was ordained a priest of the diocese of Houma-Thibadoux in Louisiana on 14 May 2004. P.J. is the son of 'Tommo' and Gertie Madden, Brackernagh, and was, for many years, a psychiatric nurse and stalwart of the nursing union. He studied for the priesthood after the death of his wife, Mary, in 1999; she was a great source of inspiration for him. *(Photo courtesy of Angela Donoghue)*

Above: Opening day, Portiuncula Hospital, 9 April 1945. Front row: Owen Larkin (contractor), Mother Margaret, Bishop Dignan, Mother Frances. Back row: Mr Kenny (consultant engineer), Fr Oliver OFM (Merchant's Quay), Msgr. Joyce, Mr H. Byrne (architect). *(Photo courtesy of FMDM Archives)*

Left: Garda Pat Ryan and a commercial traveller 'pose' for the camera at the top of the Market Square, c. 1955. *(Photo courtesy of Noel Ryan)*

Above and below: Dubarry Mass – staff and townspeople commemorate the new statue of Our Lady on the occasion of its blessing in the grounds of Dubarry factory, then located on Sarsfield Road. Formerly, the building was used as the old fever hospital and is now a supermarket. *(Photo courtesy of Joe Kelly)*

Qualifying as a doctor in 1947, Michael Kennedy (1918-2002) worked in Newport for seven years before moving to Ballinasloe. He married Eithne Holloway, whose father, John, was a businessman on Main Street, and one of the founders of the Ballinasloe Choral and Orchestral Society. A highly respected local physician, he was a native of Tuam. In 1824, *Pigot's Directory* records Ballinasloe as having two doctors, 'Wm. Colohan, Main Street' and 'Mr Francis Kelly, Brackney [sic]' and two surgeons, 'W.C. Barrett of the Galway Militia, Main Street' and 'Andrew Home, Main Street'. *(Photo courtesy of Eithne Kennedy)*

Staff of St Brigid's Psychiatric Hospital c. 1940: the Miss Marple-like figure on the wicker chair (central) is Dr Ada English (1873-1944). She graduated in 1903 from the Royal University as one of Ireland's first female psychiatrists. A formidable personality and ardent Nationalist, she was elected to the Dáil in May 1921 as one of the N. U. I. deputies. She came to Ballinasloe in 1904 and was appointed resident medical superintendent of St Brigid's in 1938. In her early days, she campaigned successfully to get the Galway Arms emblazoned on the buttons of the staff uniforms in place of Queen Victoria. The man in the Roman collar to her right is Fr William Cummins (1906-1973) while the senior clergyman is Fr Edward Hughes (1897-1964) who was Adm. at the time. *(Photo courtesy of Liam Kelly)*

Thomas D'Arcy (1879-1951) and his wife Jane (née Riddell) (1904-1997). Thomas was a tailor in Bill Crichton's and later in Evan's with other tailors like Henry O'Halloran, Jack Riddell, Willie Donnellan and Bill Killucan. An Urban District councillor for a number of years, he and Jane reared eleven children in a small house in St Michael's Square, before moving to Harbour Road.
They had twelve children, forty-two grandchildren and seventy-two great-grandchildren. *(Photo courtesy of Helen D'Arcy)*

Four generations of D'Arcys: Jane D'Arcy with her son Brian, granddaughter Maria and great-granddaughter, baby Zoe. *(Photo courtesy of Helen D'Arcy)*

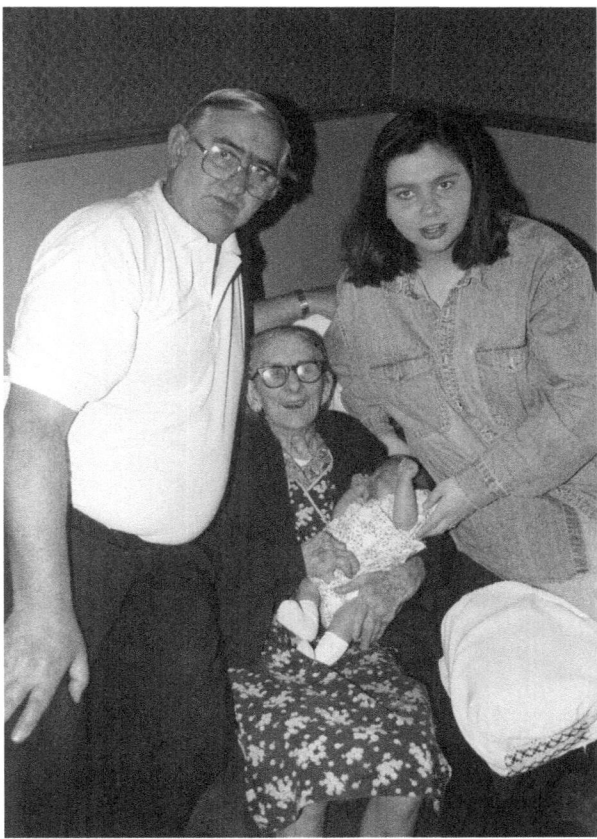

A somewhat disagreeable-looking Bishop Thomas O'Dea (not looking at the camera) takes centre stage in this scene, outside the Bishop's palace in Loughrea in 1910. To his right is the slightly shorter Dr Thomas Gilmartin, newly elected Bishop of Clonfert. At Dr Gilmartin's right shoulder, however, is Fr Johnny Heenan (1860-1931), a legend in Ballinasloe and, at that time, Adm. in Loughrea. Born on Main Street above a drapery shop (now part of Gullane's Hotel), he was ordained for Clonfert diocese in 1883. He never attained the position of P.P. as his independent-minded manner fell foul of successive bishops. His personal donation of £5 in 1923 funded the local Choral and Orchestral Society's maiden production, *Trial by Jury*. The conductor was Lavinia Sheridan, LISM – these letters indicated 'Licentiate of the Italian School of Music' but Heenan redubbed her 'Little Irish Singing Machine'.

Sadly, he became the victim of acute rheumatoid arthritis and by 1930 he had completely lost the use of his limbs. As a consequence, he would frequently hear confession outside of a confessional box, when the practice was not customary, due to his inability to draw in his legs. His sister, Annie, became a teacher at the workhouse school where his mother was matron.

While stories about him are legion, the most memorable concerns his sermon on hell during a particularly fearsome thunderstorm. At the climax of his homily, a bolt of lightning to St Michael's was accompanied by the 'mother and father of all thunderclaps'. Apparently, people screamed in terror, giving Fr Heenan tremendous satisfaction at the conclusion of the lesson! *(Photo courtesy of Clonfert Diocesan Archive)*

With the old Munster and Leinster bank in the background, dignitaries commemorate the 50th anniversary of the insurrection in 1966. Left to right: Monsignor Thomas Fahy, Fr Peter Dunne, Adm., Monsignor Timothy Glennon, Dean Cyril Champ, Tadhg MacLochlainn and Patrick Carroll. Carroll, who was a court clerk, had been the first to read the 1916 Proclamation outside the town hall and was arrested for the privilege. Here, he re-enacts that occasion. Tadhg MacLochlainn (1906-1999), though a native of Killure in Fohenagh parish, is readily identified with Ballinasloe, having produced eight books on its local history, most notably, *Ballinasloe: Inniu agus Inné*. In 1930, he returned from England where he had worked for four years and got a job as a social assistance officer. At the end of his long and remarkable life, he was chiefly responsible for the Famine Remembrance Park at 'Bullies Acre', opposite the old 'A.T. Cross' factory in Deerpark. This had been the mass grave for victims of the Famine. *(Photo courtesy of Patricia Carroll)*

Pat Galvin, who began teaching in the new St Grellan's boys' national school in 1937, having taught at the old boys' school for ten years, which was located at the rear of the town hall. A native of Ballygar, he came to Ballinasloe at the time of the Rising and involved himself in many aspects of community life. He served at different times on Ballinasloe Urban Council and on Galway County Council from 1955-79. He was prominent in community affairs, helping the town receive a Tidy Towns National Award in 1977. He was also involved in the Social Centre and the establishment of a heated indoor swimming pool. He died in 1987. *(Photo courtesy of Anna Goode)*

Willie Bruce (RIP), Eddie Moran and Paddy Moran (RIP) outside the headquarters of the fire station, situated near the Fair Green. The Morans came to Ballinasloe when Paddy and Eddie's father, who was in the army, married Mary Brennan from Harbour Road. A kind, friendly and witty man, Paddy Moran served with the fire brigade for thirty years.

One of the best known of the fire-brigade officers in Ballinasloe was Jack Carrig who headed up the unit when it was formed locally in 1940. Twenty years before Steve McQueen and co. were pretending to fight 'the towering inferno', Jack Carrig and his men were gallantly battling the blaze that engulfed the old workhouse on Society Street. The town owes heroic men like Jack Carrig and Paddy Moran a deep debt of gratitude. *(Photo courtesy of Helen D'Arcy)*

On the occasion of Garda Pat Ryan's retirement from the force. *(Photo courtesy of Helen Maguire)*

Jubilant homecoming scene at the top of St Michael's on Market Square. *(Photo courtesy of Martin Ryan)*

Paddy Beegan, T.D., a native of Oatfield in the parish of Aughrim, was elected to the Dáil in 1932, having joined the Volunteers in 1917 and the South Galway Brigade of the I.R.A. in the battle for independence. Taking the Republican side at the treaty, he was imprisoned from August 1922 until December 1923.

A farmer by occupation, he had joined Fianna Fáil from its formation and was parliamentary secretary to the Minister for Finance at the time of his sudden death, aged sixty-one, on 2 February 1958. He was hugely popular in Ballinasloe. On the by-election caused by his death, his nephew, Tony Miller, was elected T.D. *(Photo courtesy of Gerry Miller)*

Dermot Staunton, owner of The Countryman Pub and late of Creagh, shares a joke with a passer-by. *(Photo courtesy of Michael Staunton)*

Ballinasloe's current Lord Mayor, Michael Kelly, who is a native of the town, with his wife, Anne, and daughter, Niamh. Mike's parents, Tony and Phil, were much-loved residents of the town. Tony was a familiar face in the annual Choral Society's productions. Mike's brother, Joe, runs the popular Joe's Bar on Society Street. *(Photo courtesy of U.D.C.)*

'The Billiards Club' outside 'The Hut' c. 1945. *(Photo courtesy of F. Walsh)*

Patrick Hogan (1891-1936), Minister for Agriculture (1922-1932), was a solicitor by profession in town. This firm is still practicing under his name, though owned by Glynn's. He also had practices in Loughrea, Ballygar and Mountbellew. He was considered an exemplary minister and was responsible for the formation of the Land Commission in 1923. A strong advocate of the Treaty prior to the Civil War, he was to become a sharp critic of de Valera. He was also an opponent of the revival of the Irish language, feeling it a foolhardy project outside of Gaeltacht areas where the active support of the people was absent. His career was cut tragically short following a car accident in the village of Aughrim. An oft-quoted motto of his was:

One More Sow,
And One More Cow,
One More Acre, Under the Plough.

In one celebrated incident during a public meeting, a heckler shouted out:
  'Mr Hogan, how many toes has a pig?'
  To which Hogan replied:
  'Take off your boots and count them!' *(Photo courtesy of Brigid Hogan-O'Higgins)*

1970: Fr Peter Dunne, Adm., leads parishioners from town on a pilgrimage to Lourdes. *(Photo courtesy of Phil Bruce)*

Above: Willie Bruce (1940-1996) with his wife, Phil. Willie was a mechanic and a member of the local fire-brigade service. Phil is the only person in town who now knows 'The Ballad of Jack Keogh', and sang in the '70s and '80s with a popular local band 'The Western Rovers', also featuring Frankie Walsh, Jimmy Reilly, Ollie Glennon, Frank Hession and Gabriel Donnellan. *(Photo courtesy of Phil Bruce)*

Left: A well-known figure in the town's twentieth-century history, Jack Keogh was imprisoned on a number of occasions for his militant Republican activities. He made a celebrated escape on one occasion from the Dundrum Prison Hospital, commemorated in the 'Ballad of Jack Keogh', a.k.a. 'The Galway Rebel'. He married and lived in Chicago for some years where, on one occasion, there was an attempt on his life. He returned to Ireland in the late thirties, and died in 1945. *(Photo courtesy of Phil Bruce)*

Miss Sheridan, or 'Breezy', holding her trademark baton, pictured with the orchestra of the Ballinasloe Choral Society, after a production of *The Geisha Girl*. *(Photo courtesy of Garbally College Archives)*

Lord Mayor, Andrew Jennings, invests the King. *(Photo courtesy of Dan Spain)*

Above: One of Ballinasloe's evergreen natives, Joe Higgins, with his wife Phil. From Emmet Place, Joe's contribution to light entertainment in the town has been unequalled over the years. While working in Dubarry Shoe Factory he founded the Dubarry Choral Society, also writing and producing its shows, with everything from pantomime to revue. In 1956, he became Ballinasloe's first 'King of the Fair', a tradition only recently revived. For the 'coronation' ceremony, he was escorted down the Grand Canal on a barge and greeted by around 30,000 cheering spectators – a bigger crowd than that which welcomed Cardinal Wiseman in 1858! His aides-de-camp on that occasion were Joe Brennan (RIP) and Jimmy Greally.

Though he was initially hesitant to accept the position, Joe threw himself into his ambassadorial role with characteristic gusto, opening local dances and events. On one occasion, he gave an impromptu half-day to the students at the convent school while on a visit, to the delight of the students but the consternation of the nuns! Today, Joe is retired but can still be found energetically walking around Brackernagh, being greeted by fellow natives of the town, who are fully aware of his great contribution to their lives. *(Photo courtesy of Joe Higgins)*

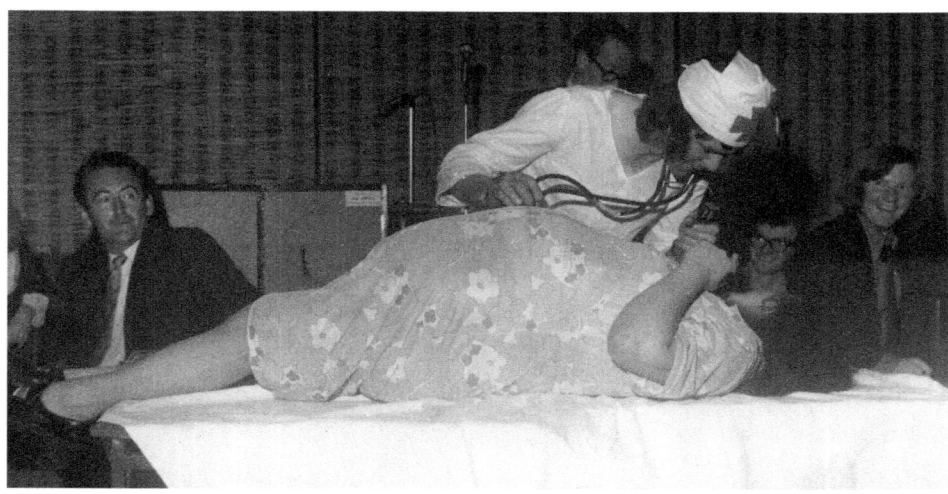

Opposite below: 'Dr' Willie Devlin examines a very expectant 'patient', Phil Lloyd, during a charity concert in Hayden's Hotel which was scripted by Joe Higgins. Frankie Walsh and friends look on in bemusement. *(Photo courtesy of Phil Bruce)*

Right: Pat Stack (1925-1997). In 1962, he was appointed secretary to the Galway/Roscommon Mental Health Board which had its headquarters at St Brigid's Hospital. A real gentleman in every respect, he had a distinguished service record with the Local Authority and Health Services until his retirement in 1988. St Brigid's was founded by the Lord Lieutenant of Ireland in 1833 and was the first attempt of its kind to address the question of psychiatric illness in the west of Ireland. Though early methods of treatment would now be seen as primitive and, occasionally, downright barbaric, for its time it was a new venture. It was people like Pat Stack and the many dedicated staff who nursed and worked within its walls, that helped to turn mental health services into a modern, caring practice. *(Photo courtesy of Martin Stack)*

Below: 'Strike up the Band': Dubarry Choral Society, c. 1970s. *(Photo courtesy of Frankie Walsh)*

'Stepping it out' at a Dubarry Choral Society presentation in the town hall c. 1970. Left to right: Jack Hall, Timmy Casey, Michael Gilligan, Frankie Walsh, Martin Murray, Peter Keighery. *(Photo courtesy of Frankie Walsh)*

St Stephen's Day, 1971, brings some post-Christmas revellers down Society Street. *(Photo courtesy of F. Walsh)*

Above left: Mr Rory Kilduff, Main Street, has seen much come and go in his eighty-five years. *(Photo courtesy of Una Spain)*

Above right: Denis Egan, one of Ballinasloe's early sport stars of the twentieth century. A native of Derrymullen, he married Bridget Connaire from Kilclooney, who was a sister of Mick Connaire. He played for Galway in the 1934 and 1938 All-Irelands. Denis was only in his forties when he lost his life to peritonitis. He was the first patient to die on the operating table in Portiuncula Hospital. *(Photo courtesy of Tina Earls)*

Right: Denis Egan's daughter Mary Earls was a great inspiration to the family business and, with her husband Vincent, a local builder, undertook major projects such as providing the town with new civic offices and the Marina Point development nearby. A popular citizen, she died in 2002. *(Photo courtesy of Tina Earls)*

Joe Higgins' father-in-law was Christy Regan (1903-1998), also a native of Ballinasloe, who was educated at the old Tea Lane school and worked as a postman. Christy spent his early days in the army and was stationed at the barracks Michael Collins visited just hours before his death in 1922. *(Photo courtesy of Joe Higgins)*

The King salutes. *(Photo courtesy of Dan Spain)*

Judge Oliver Macklin (1920-1994) was a native of Athleague, Co. Roscommon. He enrolled as a solicitor in 1948 and was made a judge in 1974. Appointed president of the district court in 1985, he retired in 1990. No one who ever met him could help but be influenced by his decency and gentle Christian manner. He wore his erudition lightly and is remembered with admiration by many. The firm of Fair and Murtagh, with which he is closely associated, is today a thriving legal practice. The entry for Ballinasloe in *Slater's Directory* of 1846 states, 'Petty sessions are held every Wednesday and Saturday in a courthouse attached to the brideswell'. At that time, the town could boast of four 'attorneys', listed as 'Messrs. Edward Blake (River Street), Malachi Keogh (River Street & 2 N. Cumberland Street Dublin), Peter McDonogh (Dunlo Street & 16 Holles Street Dublin) and William Wallace (River Street)'. *(Photo courtesy of Ciara Macklin.)*

Bracken's Pub and Grocery with the proprietor, P.J. Bracken, standing outside. Located on the lower end of Dunlo Street, it is now a restaurant. At the turn of the century, many public houses doubled as groceries and were 'two-a-penny'. A sign over one pub at the time of the First World War read, 'After two pints of Guinness, life doesn't look quite so bad!' *(Photo courtesy of Gerry Stronge)*

Dr Padraic Gullane, a native of Main Street, who is lionised by his peers in the medical profession as an eminent ear, nose and throat surgeon. His parents ran The Log Cabin on Main Street for many years. It is now better known as Gullane's Hotel, and is owned and managed by his brother Tomás. His other siblings, Anna and Eamon, have their own successful careers. *(Photo courtesy of Tomás Gullane)*

Mrs Julia McKenna of Brackernagh was legendary for her kindness and hospitality. Her daughter was Mrs Lily Broderick, who served the town for many years on the Urban District Council. *(Photo courtesy of Mrs Lily Broderick)*

Michael, Maureen and Liam Keller enjoy a social evening in 1957. Sadly, Michael died as a young man. The Keller's have strong links with Loughrea, their forebears have done much of the excellent timberwork in St Brendan's Cathedral. *(Photo courtesy of Anne Curtin)*

Post-office staff on the occasion of a retirement presentation c. 1970s. *(Photo courtesy of Enda Jennings)*

Very Revd Lt. Col. Daniel J. McHugh, O.B.E. When the First World War broke out, many Ballinasloe men generously gave their lives in the fight against the Kaiser. After Bishop Gilmartin of Clonfert appealed for priests to do likewise, the first man to volunteer was Fr Dan McHugh (1880-1961). He had been a native of Knockroon House, Headford, and was a curate locally. He continued to serve in the armed forces as chaplain until his retirement in the forties. He is buried in the Franciscan cemetery in the town of Milford-on-Sea. *(Photo courtesy of Fr Declan Kelly, private collection)*

Emer, David and Fiona Duane, grandchildren of Gerard (RIP) and Caitlin Duane, and all talented musicians in their own right. *(Photo courtesy of Joe Duane)*

Above: Chariot bearing King Joe as he waves to his subjects. *(Photo courtesy of Dan Spain)*

Right: The King's boat docks. *(Photo courtesy of Dan Spain)*

Above: Mattie Giblin crowned while Tadhg MacLochlainn commentates. *(Photo courtesy of Dan Spain)*

Left: King of the Fair, Mattie Giblin, led by Jack Guinnessy in a top hat. *(Photo courtesy of Dan Spain)*

The King reflects ... *(Photo courtesy of Dan Spain)*

Fr John Kelly, Adm., with parishioners after saying a station Mass. *(Photo courtesy of Dan Spain)*

'Pay homage to your King.' *(Photo courtesy of Dan Spain)*

Friends gather in the Log Cabin. *(Photo courtesy of Dan Spain)*

Above left: Dan Spain, John Fletcher and friend, on Main Street. *(Photo courtesy of Dan Spain)*

Above right: Bridie Dolan and May Spain at the top of the Square. *(Photo courtesy of Dan Spain)*

A lovely day for Guinness ... ADC Joe Brennan (RIP) stands guard over the King. *(Photo courtesy of Dan Spain)*

Dan Spain and Willie Divilly square up to one another. *(Photo courtesy of Dan Spain)*

Jack Guinnessy leads his charges around Hill's Corner. *(Photo courtesy of Dan Spain)*

Above left: The old and the new … a Fair Day parade. *(Photo courtesy of Dan Spain)*

Above right: Timmy Divilly and May Spain trip the light fantastic as a young Tomas Gullane looks on. *(Photo courtesy of Dan Spain)*

Fresh fish – a market day in Ballinasloe. *(Photo courtesy of Dan Spain)*

Taking a stroll on Society Street. *(Photo courtesy of Dan Spain)*

Corpus Christi procession down Dunlo Street c. 1950s. *(Photo courtesy of Dan Spain)*

'And mine's a pint!' Annual vintners' outing c. 1970 *(Photo courtesy of Martin Ryan)*

Relays' 1984 production of Brian Friel's *Translations*, directed by Eamonn O'Donoghue. Front row (left to right): Barry Lally, Mike O'Reilly, Maeve D'Arcy, _____, John Boland. Second row (left to right): Joe Bergin, Geraldine Moran, Tony D'Arcy (RIP), Dominic Divilly.

(Photo courtesy of Barry Lally)

Relays' 1984 production of John McClure's *Private Wars*, directed by Eamonn O'Donoghue. From left to right: Dominic Divilly, Eamonn O'Donoghue, Hugh Kirwin, Mike Donegan. *(Photo courtesy of Barry Lally)*

St Brigid's Christmas concert group (drama section) in the 1960s. From left to right: Gerry Hurley, Mike Coleman, Kitty Kynes (née Manning), Seán Tully, Kitty Wade (now Cahill), Mickie Costello (RIP), Mary Manning (now Dooley), Renée Clogher (now Ryan), Martin Hynes. *(Photo courtesy of Barry Lally)*

Right: A scene from Ballinasloe Street Theatre's 1987 production of *Everyman*, directed by Barry Lally. From left to right: Kevin Boland, Barry Lally. *(Photo courtesy of Barry Lally)*

Below: St Brigid's Dramatic Society's 1981 production of Teresa Deevy's *The King of Spain's Daughter*, directed by Barry Lally. Front Row (left to right): Teresa Lyons, Mary Teresa Hession. Second Row (left to right): Noel McHugh, Paddy Seale, Pat Clark. *(Photo courtesy of Barry Lally)*

Left: One of the many 'good Samaritans' to grace Ballinasloe, Hilda Bradley (née Mathies), she was a native of Cologne, Germany. In 1922 she married John Bradley and moved to Ireland four years later. Before the existence of the St Vincent de Paul Society, this lady often dropped off parcels of food at the doors of Ballinasloe's needy without so much as a word. *(Photo courtesy of Phil Bruce)*

Above left: Paddy Manton (1924-1999), who hailed from Kilrickle but lived most of his life in Creagh. One of the many greats to pass through the town's corridor of sporting history, he played on the victorious Loughrea minor hurling team of 1942 and, in 1951, became a forward on the Ballinasloe senior hurling team, helping to win the county title in the same year. He played alongside names such as Inky Flaherty, Jimmy Creaven, Staff Ruane and Tommy Larkin. Paddy was a psychiatric nurse in St Brigid's Hospital. *(Photo courtesy of Gretta Costello)*

Above right: Douglas Rafter, Main Street, seen in 1964 in his role in *Calamity Jane*. *(Photo courtesy of Davey Rafter)*

Opposite below: Third class (1949), St Grellan's national school. Front row (left to right): Dermot McMurrough, Pat Lennon, Lynch, Kevin Cummins, Bill Colohan. Second row (left to right): Connolly, Barnes, Bernard Ryan, Brian Croghan, _____, Regan, Oliver McGahon, Jackie Clarke, 'Spon' Cunnane. Third row (left to right): Séamus O'Connor, Liam Smyth, Gabriel Kiely, Jimmy Jarvis, Connor, Austin Kiely, Cregg, _____, Finnerty, Hodgins, Barry Lally. Fourth row (left to right): Pádraic Clarke, _____, Bernard O'Beirne, 'Buddy' Donnellan, Tony Fahy, Pat MacDonnell, Brian Connaughton, Bernard Murray, Tommy Ryan, _____, George Walker.
Fifth row (left to right): 'Bevin' Griffin, _____, Dempsey, Holian, Alfie Blundell, _____, Murphy, _____, Carr, Tommy Goggins.

(Photo courtesy of Barry Lally)

Goods friends… Tom Joe Kelly, Austin Whelan, Johnny Furey, Seán O'Flynn, Johnny Furey and J.J. Hyland. Seán O'Flynn ran The Leinster House, a popular pub on Main Street, which had acquired its name from the many political 'tête-à-têtes' waged therein. Johnny Furey was a hugely popular figure locally. He was greatly involved in the Choral Society, the last show he participated in being *The Merry Widow* (1973). He died in 1989. *(Photo courtesy of Davey Rafter)*

The Western Rovers' Showband. *(Photo courtesy of Phil Bruce)*

Above: A fondly remembered resident of Portnick, Terry Maguire at his son John's graduation. Terry worked as an accountant at Bórd Na Móna in nearby Shannonbridge. Up to the present day, many residents of the town choose to supplement their oil/heating resources by cutting turf. Now mostly done by machine, up to recent enough times, it was cut by hand-sleán. Due to the Earl of Clancarty's eminent societal status, Ballinasloe was spared no expense when it came to improvements and received gas-lighting as a town in 1841. This system served the public streets until 1943. Indeed, for many years, Nicholas E. O'Carroll, proprietor of the local paper, *The East Galway Democrat*, wrote a gossip column entitled 'Under the Lamp'. *(Photo courtesy of Helen Maguire)*

Right: Harry, father of the Lloyd family, was known for his great neighbourliness and earned the name 'the Poolboy Councillor'. His daughter, Lucy Lloyd-Keighery, was elected to the Urban District Council in 1998 and has served the town as Lord Mayor. Mrs Lloyd had been Nora Madden from Deerpark. *(Photo courtesy of Phil Bruce)*

Richie Walsh, in his celebrated role of the judge in the *Trial of Old Mother Reilly*. Written by Joe Higgins, who also played the part of the eponymous and hysterical Irish washerwoman, it was performed in many places. Sadly, Richie, died at the young age of forty-six. *(Photo courtesy of Frankie Walsh)*

Richie Walsh. *(Photo courtesy of Frankie Walsh)*

Pointing to the future, Ballinasloe's latest development, the Carlton Shearwater Hotel. *(Photo courtesy of Carlton Shearwater Hotel)*